MARY EMMERLING'S

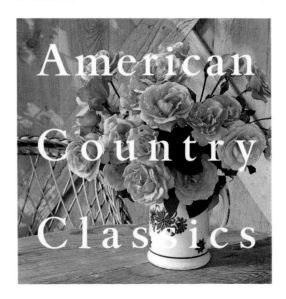

American Country Classics

MARY EMMERLING'S

American

Country

Classics

THE NEW AMERICAN COUNTRY LOOK

Text by Carol Sama Sheehan

Photographs by Chris Mead

Clarkson Potter / Publishers, New York

To All of Our Country Friends

Published by Clarkson N. Potter, Inc.,
distributed by Crown Publishers, Inc.,
201 East 50th Street, New York, New York 10022

CLARKSON N. POTTER,
POTTER and colophon are trademarks
of Clarkson N. Potter, Inc.

Manufactured in Japan

Design by Howard Klein

Library of Congress Cataloging-in-Publication Data

Emmerling, Mary Ellisor.
[American country classics]
Mary Emmerling's American country classics / text by
Carol Sama Sheehan : photographs by Chris Mead.
1. Decoration and ornament, Rustic—United States.
2. Interior decoration—United States.
I. Sheehan, Carol Sama. II. Title. III. Title: American country classics.
NK2002. E466   1990   747.213—dc20   89-71099
                                                              CIP
ISBN 0-517-57168-4
10 9 8 7 6 5 4 3 2 1
First Edition

Dear Friends,

American Country Classics is very special to me. It has been ten years since my first book, *American Country,* was published in 1980. Since that time, many more fans have come to admire and collect American Country. *American Country Classics* is a special celebration of this enduring style— a guide to how America really lives.

With special thanks to:

Don Kelly and Warren Fitzsimmons for always helping me; Annie Degeurin for introducing me to the Kennedys; Robert and Joy Lewis for all the extra help; Buffy Birrittella for a special friendship.

To all those who are in *American Country Classics.* I wouldn't have a book without these special friends: Buffy Birrittella, Ryan Carey and Mac McLean, Bruce and Andrea Dern, Peggy Drexler, Tam and Nora Jane Etheridge, Tom Fallon, Patrick and Elizabeth Gerschel, John and Marilyn Hannigan, John and Sandy Horvitz, Michael and Eleanore Kennedy, Robert Kinnaman and Brian Ramaekers, Robert and Joy Lewis, Stephen Mack, De and Paul Madden, Leonard and Adele Pack, Derald and Janet Ruttenberg, George Schoellkopf and Ron Johnson, Joel Schumacher, Eugenie Voorhees, Thomas K. Woodard and Blanche Greenstein, and Lynda and Peter Guber.

To Joshua Greene for the beautiful photographs.

To Nancy Novogrod and *HG.*

Always, special love to my family: my mother, Marthena Ellisor; my children, Samantha and Jonathan; and my brother, Terry.

To Chris Mead, who is still my best friend and the best photographer in the whole world.

To Carol Sama Sheehan, whose writing I love; Larry Sheehan for his help with everything; and Aurelie Sheehan for helping to get the book in on time.

To everyone involved in all my books. I will always be grateful again and again to my agents Gayle Benderoff and Deborah Geltman and to all those at Clarkson N. Potter and Crown Publishers: first to Lauren Shakely, who is the best editor and friend; Howard Klein for the most wonderful book design; Carol Southern; Alan Mirken; Bruce Harris; Pam Reycraft for helping me with the directory and the organization; Amy Schuler; Laurie Stark; Mark McCauslin; Joan Denman; Michelle Sidrane; Phyllis Fleiss; Jo Fagan; Barbara Marks and Hilary Bass in Publicity, who do everything to help me; Gail Shanks and everyone else on the Crown sales force, who make all my books best sellers.

To all a big thanks!

M.E.

◣ Contents

WHEN DO YOU THINK THE FAD WILL be over?" someone asked me shortly after the publication of *American Country*. That volume was the first book to help people bring painted chests, corner cupboards, ladder-back chairs, quilts, baskets, rag rugs, and folk art into their homes in what is now known as the country style. "I'm not sure it will ever be over," I replied, "and I know it's not a fad!"

In my own experience I had already learned that American Country was both versatile and enduring—a genuine national treasure, like baseball or jazz. My travels throughout the United States in the past decade have borne that out. The purpose of *American Country Classics* is to show readers the classic elements of country style as expressed in inspiring personal interpretations. On the practical level, the book illustrates how country

style can work for any family, no matter how casual or formal its life-style, with regional accents as different as the New England quilt and the Navajo blanket, in settings as diverse as a log cabin or a beach house.

To me, American Country represents the most comfortable and meaningful identity one could ◼ *Introduction* ever hope to achieve for one's home. My quest for that "look"—although it is much more than a look—began when I was a newlywed in my first New York apartment. Working at a fashion magazine, I dutifully decorated with chrome, glass, and velvet, elements considered by that magazine to be essentials of the chic interior of the day. It looked contemporary, but it was disquietingly cool for all its high style, especially for a small-town person.

I had collected Archie comics, not antiques, as a girl, but I was always an avid museum-goer. Trips to the Smithsonian Institution, Williamsburg, Monticello, and Mount Vernon had instilled in me an unconscious appreciation for rooms that evoked our American heritage. I even had a blood connection with that past, with two presidents, William Henry Harrison and Benjamin Harrison, in our family tree. Ironically, I grew up surrounded by "suites" of shiny new reproduction furniture, instead of the historic family heirlooms the two chief executives had once used. They had been appropriated for an official Harrison museum in Indiana.

That winter, on a ski trip to Vermont, and without really knowing why, I indulged in an antiquing

spree and took home a truckload of bargain-priced golden oak cupboards, tables, and chairs. The old pieces looked surprisingly wonderful in the apartment and even proved to be compatible with the fancy modern gear. The next thing I knew, my mother was calling me "wacko" for paying $300 for a red-painted dry sink at an antiques fair.

Coincidentally, the American Bicentennial Celebration was upon us. Earlier, I had savored the skill and whimsy of early American craftsmen at an exhibit of folk art in the Whitney Museum of American Art in New York City. Now, with the country's history in the spotlight, I became aware that an important part of our past, in the form of folk art, furniture, handcrafts, and discarded tools and implements, was scattered willy-nilly in attics, barns, antiques shops, flea market stalls, swap meets, and tag

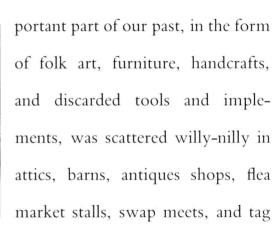

sales. My growing collection of business cards and scribbled names eventually became the basis for the directories included in *American Country,* a resource that allowed people to find the same treasures for their homes that I had discovered for mine.

Whereas *American Country* outlined the fundamentals of our native style, the present volume shows how American Country is expressed most successfully in a wide variety of dwellings. In homes where the setting may be Traditional, Romantic, Rustic, or Eclectic, the common link is a cherished appreciation for the furniture, art, and appurtenances of the historic eras in which our country was founded, settled, and pioneered. Warmth, comfort, and tradition are the classic components of the style.

I have come to realize that country style is truly a movable feast. I have taken my country furniture with me from that original boxy city apartment, first to a sophisticated commercial loft, then to an antique farmhouse, then a tropical Victorian cottage, and finally to a brand-new beach house. (I say "finally," but we are planning another move in the not-so-distant future!) The point is, to my lasting satisfaction, the furniture has adapted beautifully to each location. My $300 dry sink has served with distinction as a wet bar, buffet, or potting table, depending on the needs of each house. You just can't make mistakes with these simple, charming pieces.

While this book demonstrates that type of versatility over and over again, it also reveals how country style is at home in virtually any kind of architecture, the hallmark of classical design. Even more important, it suits a wide spectrum of personal taste and individual expression. Today, the conventional image of country is that of a New England saltbox filled with dark wood, hooked rugs, and slipware, but there is more than one way to fill a corner cupboard. I happen to have a weakness for hearts and old toolboxes, but it is not so much what you collect, as how you enjoy the collections. If I gave the same barnful of country furnishings to the imaginative people who live in the homes featured in this book, each of them would use it to achieve her or his own distinctive country look.

An Indian weaver of the Southwest traditionally includes a tiny flaw in the pattern of the rug she is making, to ensure that the gods, who are the only perfect beings, know she does not presume to be perfect herself. All country things reveal that kind of humble personal signature. Miles Carpenter, who sold watermelon out of his roadside icehouse in Virginia, started carving wood slices of the melon to pass the time. Each slice was different, and by the time he was ninety, Miles was a famous folk artist who had inspired many collectors as well as copycats.

Humble as a footstool or proud as a Windsor chair, the arts and artifacts of country style are special because they carry the unique stamp of their maker. The new country look is simply the best of the old. Time, the ultimate test of a classic style, has bestowed its stamp of approval upon this expressive, flexible, and enduring home genre.

T HE PUREST INTERPRETATION OF AMERICAN COUNTRY IS found in dwellings dating back to the earliest days of the Republic, containing furnishings and folk art of the era. Built by settlers using native wood and stone, the houses more often than not consist of a floor plan of small rooms, huddled around the life-giving warmth of primitive hearths and illuminated, but only barely, by tiny-paned windows. *Traditional* Unlike museums, these houses are surprisingly livable and alive today. Homes of more recent vintage achieve a sense of history by remaining true to the customs and crafts of a time and region. The most venerable houses, concentrated, not surprisingly, along the Eastern Seaboard, make up an important part of our heritage, all the more precious as their numbers diminish. In preserving these old buildings, their owners not only have made wonderful homes for themselves, they have saved a bit of our mutual past.

Robert and Joy Lewis

THE SMALLEST HOUSE IN THE PICTURESQUE OLD whaling village of Sag Harbor, originally a tiny waterfront ship's store built in 1750, is one of the community's richest in Revolutionary artifacts. Over the front door flies a replica of the six-pointed Stars and Stripes, a local pennant of independence predating the Betsy Ross flag. On the grounds stand healthy specimens of three traditional decora- ◣ *Sag Harbor, Long Island* tive American trees—franklinia, holly, and magnolia—overlooking beds of fragrant heirloom varieties of roses, herbs, heliotrope, foxgloves, hollyhocks, morning glories, and other annuals and perennials.

Lovingly restored, the house is both a fascinating piece of American history and a refuge that offers comfort without doing injury to tradition.

"A shipwreck is always intriguing, especially when it's in your own basement," says designer Robert Lewis. He is referring to the root cellar, constructed with salvaged wooden ship sheathing, that he and his wife Joy discovered under their historic Sag Harbor house a few years ago. The entire building was something of a wreck at the time. "It was almost into the ground," Joy recalls, but by digging into the social and architectural history of the area, as well as literally digging at the site, the Lewises soon found its secret past. "You see the plaster on the walls, looking as if it had been patty-caked on by hand, and it gives you such a strong feeling of an earlier time," Joy observes.

The couple decided to preserve the dwelling as a small home rather than impose a major enlargement, which would have disturbed its essential character. Robert drew on both his infatuation with Bauhaus design philosophy and love of early American simplicity to complete the transformation. Outside, Lewis, a lifelong gardener, turned the tiny backyard into a big outdoor room, paving it with brick and planting perimeter beds with trees, flowers, and herbs that might have flourished there 200 years ago. Inside, he kept the 18th-century structure, introducing modern amenities by removing the "decaying 20th-century add-ons, made with chewing-gum and rubber-band construction." Superimposing his design on the original plan, he created two one-room structures for a kitchen and dining/sitting room brightened by several discreetly placed skylights.

"We didn't want to live in a museum," Joy notes, yet the couple has succeeded in bringing to life the colors and textures of another era, in a place that has become home once again.

ABOVE: A collection of 18th- and early 19th-century pieces, mixed with contemporary seating and lighting, reflects the owners' desire for "new comfort in an old setting." The pair of armchairs were made by the esteemed local furniture maker Nathaniel Dominy V (1770–1852).
OPPOSITE PAGE: In an unusual Long Island corner cupboard, a collection of English black transfer ware depicting images of the young republic is juxtaposed with other objects evoking the history of the house.

BELOW: Shards of pottery and china from 1840 and earlier, found when the original house site was excavated, make a colorful arrangement on a country table.

An unplanned "dig" under the house yielded a surprisingly rich variety of colors and patterns. Unearthed were shards of 18th-century English transfer, Chinese Export porcelain, free-blown glass, creamware, Mocha ware, and lusterware. One plate reconstructed from remnants bears the hopeful message "A reward for innocence and truth."

ABOVE: Beeswax busts of the original First Family stand among a large collection of Rockingham pottery.

LEFT: Two pairs of eyes in a portrait by Orlando Hand Bears gaze upon flotsam and jetsam of the 19th century: a French Egyptianate tin urn, a steamship of tin, a carved ivory-headed walking cane, and a length of whale's rib earmarked to be a cane but never carved.

LEFT: The porch room, habitat for an antique iron doorstop bunny, is sparely furnished with an 18th-century Irish pine cupboard, Long Island Queen Anne chairs, and a birch drop-leaf game table.

OPPOSITE PAGE: Breadboards to work dough bound for a beehive oven and hand-colored stencil prints used to illustrate a 19th-century New York seed catalog now provide food for thought in the kitchen.

RIGHT: The old staircase original to the house so resembled a ship's ladder that the owners commissioned a local craftsman to make a rope railing tied with nautical knots to accompany it.

ABOVE: A sleeping loft
remodeled in the
image of ship's quar-
ters contains a cast-iron
lighthouse night-light,
a basket of rope knots,
and a replica of the
America's Cup trophy.
A sampler of essential
ties reveals some of the
complexity of rigging
a sailing vessel.

OPPOSITE PAGE: A
flea market flag col-
lection makes a star-
spangled salute from
a gathering basket of
oak splints.

George Schoellkopf
and Ron Johnson

A 1750 SALTBOX IN THE HILLS OF SOUTHERN NEW England houses a collection of kitchenware dating from the early days of the United States. The house belongs to antiques dealer George Schoellkopf and the landscape painter Ron Johnson, who share a passion for the aesthetic values of that period. Slipware, bearing the decorative flourishes of white clay applied by hand, and redware, its plainer cousin, are forms of low-fire

◤ *New England*

pottery using red clay. The vessels produced by this process were used for the routine domestic chores of baking, serving, and storing foods. But like all the 18th-century antiques collected in the house, each piece of pottery bears the distinctive stamp of an individual talent. George Schoellkopf is a Dallas-born collector who still owns the first antique he

26

ever bought, a Queen Anne chair he acquired when he was twelve, with $100 his grandmother had given him for Christmas. Since then, George has become a passionate enthusiast of American primitive antiques, which he describes as "so powerful, they're really like good Picassos to me, only made about one hundred years earlier."

His simple, hand-hewn farmhouse, "free of ball-and-claw formality," says George, gives him the unrestricted scope to showcase his possessions as he likes. They in turn serve to resurrect the original spirit of the dwelling, he believes, "helping me to feel the ghost of the house. Antiques themselves are like the ghosts of the region where they were made," he explains, "and they belong in their own houses. I tried putting an old Pennsylvania piece here, and it just wasn't right. New England furniture is what talks here."

Because the house is small, George pays attention to the scale of the pieces he brings home. He also assesses patina. "That's a polite word for dirt," he says. "I don't believe in cleaning things up so much they make the house look new."

With its emphasis on wood and the absence of strong light (small windows kept out the frigid New England cold), the house represents what most people would think of as authentic country style. It's the kind of house where you can't be sure what the weather is like outside or, at times, what century you're in.

George sees his redware and slipware as emblematic of the expert workmanship of the 18th century. In an era when everyone made what they needed by hand, "there was more manual dexterity, and it can be seen in the craftsmanship of the furniture, folk art, and pottery. That's why 18th-century antiques are in my blood."

OPPOSITE PAGE: In a corner of the oak-floored keeping room, a maple butterfly table is surrounded by a country sampler of chairs, including the most venerable, a 17th-century armchair with carved finials. A New England painted pine hutch displays colorful pottery in the same way it did during the time of the early settlers—out in the open for all to enjoy.

ABOVE: The 18th-century mantel, newly installed but authentic to the period, surrounds the monumental fieldstone hearth. The pine-paneled keeping room might have looked the same 200 years ago. Even the "make-do wing chair" is upholstered in a period print fabric.

LEFT: Sack-back Windsor chairs with knuckle armrests were made by Amos Dennison Allen in eastern Connecticut in the late 18th century. The chandelier, topiary standards, draped windows, and portraits of the Brockmuller children as they looked in 1827 add a sense of occasion to the dining room. ABOVE: A wing chair designed to protect the sitter from drafts of a New England winter still allows an appreciative glimpse of an array of English Delft plates.

ABOVE: A corner cupboard, usually found in the "best room" of a Connecticut central-chimney house, exhibits "best china," the traditional use for this early built-in. The ball-foot blanket chest was crafted in New England ca. 1720.

RIGHT: The pencil-post bed has a canopy of antique linen. Primitive portraits over the fireplace are flanked by a painting of *The Boston* and a patchwork black cat. The pine paneling came from another house of the same vintage.

Tam and Nora Jane Etheridge

IN THE RURAL TOWN OF ROCKPORT, Mississippi, not far from the Pearl River (once used to carry cotton to market), a vestige of the Old South remains in the form of a raised farmhouse with a welcoming front porch. Now on the National Register of Historic Places, the house was built in the years immediately preceding the Civil War, with high ceilings, tall windows, and deep porches, to make life bearable in the sultry summers. Today the

◥ *Rockport, Mississippi*

porches are still the most popular rooms in the house, for coffee in the morning, company for dinner, and afterward, while the house is cooling off, moon and star viewing and conversation with friends. Inside, a mixture of handsomely plain furnishings provides rocking-chair comfort and ease. Living here is as calming and fulfilling as a walk through the coun-

34

tryside. "It just feeds my soul to be in a place like this," exults Nora Jane Etheridge. The weekend farmhouse cottage she and her husband, Tam, discovered in southern Mississippi is merely an hour's drive from their year-round home in Jackson, but light-years removed from the pace and pressure of modern life.

Rockport on the Pearl River once bustled with barges and eight noisy saloons, but when the railroad replaced the river traffic, Rockport quickly became a sleepy river town. Today, its most exciting evening is the Sunday chicken dinner at Galilee Baptist Church, and that is exactly how Nora Jane wants it.

Whenever she hails me from the porch as I come up the front walk, I feel as if I were stepping into the pages of a Eudora Welty story. The raised structure is graced with simple Greek Revival lines, a dogtrot floor plan—to capture welcome breezes—tall windows of hand-blown glass, high-rising chimneys, and a long, wide veranda. In a simple yet dignified way, the house seems to beckon to visitors with the replenishing spirit of southern country life. With no telephone or television, and the nearest newspaper six miles away, the sense of peace is almost inevitable.

"The house helps us to simplify our life," she explains. "I've never wanted to complicate it with more than it needs. I didn't want a lot to take care of—things I would have to dust—but I did want to preserve the pristine quality." That quality was the house's personality when its two predecessors lived here, one of them, a country doctor named Alford, made the only significant alteration in the history of the dwelling, adding a spacious 20 by 24–foot "great room" to serve as both his examination room and bedroom. The physician, according to Nora Jane,

Wicker furniture from the 1880s and a country Chippendale sofa offer a choice of comforts in the commodious "great room." Quilt pieces immortalizing the local pine have been sewn into pillows and framed for the wall.

"wanted to be able to get out of bed in the middle of the night for a house call without tripping over a lot of furniture."

It was the "intrinsic integrity" of the house design that prompted the National Register of Historic Places to certify the modest dwelling. Its 12-foot ceilings, heart-of-pine floors, and wide-board tongue-and-groove interior walls all are original to the house. The dwelling was raised to avoid damage from floodwaters and to promote air circulation beneath the house.

Nora Jane's lifelong interest in houses of all kinds is revealed in her and her husband's vacationing style. When they travel, they prefer places as unexpected as a 16th-century convent. But the cottage on the Pearl River remains their favorite.

"This house is such a symbol of what once was, is no more, and never again will be," says she.

LEFT: A carpenter's hand-pieced arch frames the view of a New England trestle table and French Provincial ladder-back chairs. An old commercial sign hints of the family business while the diamond quilt design painted on the floor shows off a local painter's dexterity. RIGHT: An odds-and-ends set of chairs, buttermilk pitcher, and ironstone bowl all come in handy in this unassuming kitchen of the Deep South.

LEFT: French and Italian linens, old and new, mingle on an antique walnut blanket rack with its distinctive spool turnings.

ABOVE: A leafy tree provides the convenient blind for a bather to take in the sights while enjoying a soak in the claw-footed tub.

ABOVE: **An eat-in porch enclosed with cypress lattice features a dry sink with running water, chairs Nora Jane sat in as a child in Sunday school, and an Italian chicken for a doorstop.**
RIGHT: **The local carpenter R. L. Nichols built the fancy stairway, complete with banisters and benches, to traverse the herb garden and get to the porch.**

ABOVE: The "blue" bedroom has the traditional quilts and ticking of country.

LEFT: A new mahogany four-poster is graced with the old beauty of a New England quilt sewn with a basket pattern in the owner's favorite colors. A fireplace mantel reveals the original builder's extra care in its country Federal detailing.

Stephen Mack

CHASE HILL FARM IS A COLLECTION OF VINTAGE buildings and other rarities, on 50 rural acres near the ocean coast of Rhode Island. Here Stephen Mack not only preserves authentic architecture of the 17th and 18th centuries, but also adopts some of the life-style of colonial America. A gem in his collection, a 17th-century stone-ender house with pine clapboard siding and a massive

◥ *Chase Hill Farm, Rhode Island*

pilastered chimney, was moved from its original site in Connecticut and now serves as Stephen's office. A late 19th-century center-chimney Cape Cod serves as the main residence, and a dozen other antique homes from all over New England, disassembled and in storage, await a new future at undetermined sites. "Eighteenth-century houses have an incredibly ro-

mantic feeling," says Stephen Mack, who designs and creates estates and period homes, using 18th-century buildings threatened with demolition. He meticulously takes them apart, then oversees their reassembly on appropriate sites for clients or himself: "They are built with an elegance, strength, and simplicity of design that is so beautiful it enhances the lives of the people who live in them."

Practicing what he preaches, Stephen prefers sheep to lawn mowers at Chase Hill Farm. He splits his own wood and cooks on an open fire in the hearth nearly every night. He dines by candlelight and washes his dishes by hand. He even takes his showers outdoors when weather permits. "It's very enriching to live in this house as it was meant to be lived in," he says. "There's an earthbound aspect to it that brings me in touch with the seasons and all of nature. It helps to offset my daily business routines."

I admire the way Stephen brings color into his living space just as the original dwellers would have done, with the objects he collects and by using earthy milk paints and whitewashes that he himself has mixed to treat walls and other surfaces. An authentic rather than "cutesy colonial" surrounding is the result.

In helping new owners of his buildings to incorporate modern features, Stephen finds ways to stick to his preservationist convictions. For example, instead of installing a state-of-the-art kitchen into a house that wasn't built for it, he adds unobtrusive additions to the original structures to create the needed space.

"It's very satisfying to save these buildings from destruction," he notes, "and then put them back in context by creating estates, where, with luck, they can stand another 250 years."

OPPOSITE PAGE: The main house features a parlor with a "courting window" over the door, where 18th-century parents once kept an eye on suitors. The American mushroom chair, so named for the caplike shape of its armrests, is made of maple and ash, with black-oak split seat.

ABOVE: Nautical objects provide the theme of a Cape farmhouse. Surrounding the hearth are a carved billethead, once used to decorate the bow of an 1860 sailing vessel; an old brass ship's cannon; the model of the hull of a Newfoundland square-rigger; and a group of antique telescopes.

A 250-year-old granite sink, a 1920s porcelain gas stove, and milk-painted cabinets are the latest amenities in a kitchen created by combining an old pantry with the "borning room," where women delivered their children in colonial days. Countertops were built from antique chestnut floorboards. Old French copper pots and a 19th-century iron teakettle from Newfoundland are on the stove. Festive "everyday china," once used to brighten drab country households, includes pink lusterware, blue-bordered pearl ware, and pasteware.

ABOVE: A Nova Scotian turn schooner rests atop an English mahogany chest-on-chest from the late 1700s. Nearby, the oil painting depicts a square-rigged ship that sailed out of New England in the 19th century.

RIGHT: In the "keeping room," a wood and iron chandelier oversees a mid-18th-century English oak table and set of American ladder-back chairs of similar vintage. The chimney stack is built of layers of oak timber and granite, a technique used in the 18th century to reduce the onerous chore of cutting stone.

BELOW: An 18th-century banister-backed armchair graces the west parlor, where rare books, sailor's ditty bags, and old nautical gear are displayed.

A 1931 Model AA Ford mail-delivery truck with ash panels is Mack's choice for getting around town. The recently erected antique barn houses an inventory of 18th-century doors and raised-panel walls.

ABOVE: An 18th-century maple rope bed is surrounded by rope-handled sea chests, once used to stow sailors' belongings on long voyages. The chest at the foot of the bed sports a water-resistant canvas lid. Over the bed is a mid-19th-century shadow-box model of a New England schooner. The oak-splint basket originally stored bed feathers, wool, and flax.

OPPOSITE PAGE: From the farmhouse, the open Dutch door frames a view of the rustic stone ender office cottage.

Robert Kinnaman
and Brian Ramaekers

THE UNPRETENTIOUS BEAUTY OF THE COTTAGES of eastern Long Island is a combination of the cultural background of early American colonists and the agricultural tradition of the region. This outstanding example of that plain building style was built in the 18th century by the Osborns, a farming family who originally settled a town in the area in 1652, having migrated ◣ *Eastern Long Island* from the Massachusetts Bay Colony in search of further religious freedom and fertile fields. On the exterior, the cottage's simple lines of painted white trim accent native cedar shingle siding. Within, in small rooms that are also characteristic of the style, a collection of art and antiques echoes the graceful aesthetic. "An antique isn't worth buying unless it shows its age," says Robert Kinnaman, and

he has filled his home with objects that carry their age and provenance with the dignity of distinguished senior citizens. But he is a purist when it comes to finishes: "If a chair or table has been sanded down or slicked up, it's of no interest to me whatsoever!"

The cottage of Robert and Brian Ramaekers, who are dealers of antiques, is a welcoming house, with slipcovered furniture and walls painted the warm yellow of Long Island's fabled sunsets. Responding to the house's small scale and appreciating the sculptural quality of the humblest objects, every piece is given the space it deserves. Resisting the clutter that could so easily afflict ardent collectors in a small space, Robert and Brian have cultivated a highly expressive spareness. They really use everything they have collected, even objects that are rare and valuable. "If you like old things, you have to be willing to live with them," Robert declares, and he puts his antiques to work in daily life, many in the same way they were employed 200 years ago, when new.

Their idea of a classic is "something that does not depend on fashion of the moment or of the century to justify it. It will hold its own," he notes, "thanks to the integrity of its design, color, and form, anywhere it goes, anytime." Even fragrance can bear the stamp and quality of age for him. "In the summer," Robert observes, "the air sifting down through the fireplace fills the cottage with a kind of potpourri."

On the pilastered Federal mantelpiece is an array of salt-glazed South Carolina stoneware vases, French push-up brass candlesticks, a New England carved bird, and a Queen Anne–style mirror painted to resemble carved mahogany. The froe, a bin used originally for grain storage, was hollowed out of a sycamore log in Vermont about 1750.

LEFT: Dressed for summer, 18th-century style, chairs are wrapped and tied with handwoven Indian cotton, while the sofa is covered with the pattern pelargonium (the Latin name of the common geranium). Botanical images were painted on mattress ticking on the Indiana frontier. The tree with carved birds was fashioned in Pennsylvania in the late 18th century. The 1825 stool with bowed sides and original oxblood red paint makes a useful table. RIGHT: Blanket chest with a patriotic theme, made about 1835 in Pennsylvania, shares the hall leading to the dining room with an old earthenware jar from the Mediterranean. A French 18th-century iron grate, originally used as an open-hearth grill, serves as a decorative wall hanging.

LEFT: The hearth in the original kitchen, now a part of the dining room, was built on granite used for ship's ballast in 1780. The banister-back side chair, made in Hartford circa 1740, still bears its original Indian-red paint. The pine oval drop-leaf table, dating from the 19th century, holds a hand-blown New England compote, a brass Dutch pipe rest made about 1680, and a French candlestick of steel darkened with time.

ABOVE RIGHT: In the pastel portrait of a happy child, drawn in 1835 by an unknown New England artist, the boy wears coral beads to ward off evil spirits.

RIGHT: A collapsible corner shelf shows off an array of 17th- and 18th-century accessories.

LEFT: Shelves of the
original buttery display
treasured kitchen
objects from the past,
including English
Wedgwood creamware
monogrammed with a
French family crest and
a wooden knife box
with a heart-shaped
handle hold. On the
lower shelf are painted
candle boxes, a bowl of
marble carpet balls
used for indoor cro-
quet, and a pair of iron
planting urns. In one
urn is a beaded pin-
cushion made for
the tourist trade by
an American Indian
about 1890.
ABOVE: The profile of
the man leading with
his chin was whittled
from pine by a 19th-
century folk artist.

ABOVE: The kitchen shows off shorebird decoys and a collection of stoneware jugs once used for pickling and to store cider and vinegar. Contrasting work surfaces are supplied by a 1920s store-bought enamel-top table and a much older twig plant stand of shellacked bark.

RIGHT: Instead of a medicine cabinet, the bathroom features a circa-1820 gilt-and-sand–painted mirror and an insider's view of the human thorax—an anatomical study painted on muslin for 19th-century medical students.

John and Marilyn Hannigan

THE PORCH ON A VICTORIAN COTTAGE BORDER-
ing the eastern shore of Maryland is called the
front porch, even though it is at the back of
the house. Throughout this serene, sparsely
settled region the focus of life in the house is the bay. These waters
provide livelihood for commercial fishermen, a challenging venue for
sailors and yachtsmen, and beautiful
sunsets for stay-at-homes. Here,   ◥ *Maryland's Eastern Shore*
friendly sporting dogs roam and the most taxing diversion might be a
croquet match using mallets from the Roaring Twenties. Deliberately left
undone, the house is planned for relaxed living. Even housework is literally a breeze—brisk bay winds dust the furniture once a day. So many of
us are disappointed to find modern encroachments have forever changed

70

For exercise we play with Hatton, the couple's golden retriever, and Bo, the neighbor's black Lab, or go crabbing for Chesapeake Bay's famous blue-shelled delicacy.

The house, built in 1910 and used by a Baltimore family as a retreat for decades, is now the weekend escape for Marilyn, who has an antiques shop in Washington, D.C., and her husband. In her business Marilyn trades in "serious" 18th- and 19th-century American pieces, but she has deliberately kept her cottage as simple as possible. "The house was built as a utilitarian sleep house for people who loved to fish in the summer and go duck hunting in the fall," she explains. "To make it into anything fancier would be too much of a departure."

When Marilyn works with clients, she encourages them to respond to the sort of furniture and décor the house dictates it should have, and she did the same with her cottage.

Recognizing that the bay itself was the focal point for the house, Marilyn and John "did everything we could to bring the bay into the house," adding French doors to the living room, making it an extension of the porch, and adding an upstairs porch with French doors, to take best advantage of the spectacular view.

The rattan on the porches, dating from the 1920s and painted white, is clean and comfortable, Marilyn notes. "People aren't intimidated by it." Old duck decoys and other reminders of the region's natural history and nautical traditions also look right at home in the cottage.

"One day when descendants of the original owners came by," says Marilyn, "they told us it didn't feel as if the house had changed at all since 1910. And that's exactly what we want."

our childhood haunts, but Maryland's eastern shore, where I spent my summers as a young girl, has remained just as I have always known it. It is still rural, populated by hardworking farmers and fishermen, and by vactioners who imitate the casual life-style of their neighbors.

A visit to Marilyn and John Hannigan in their Victorian cottage in the town of St. Michaels always has an automatic calming effect on me. Life is conducted on the porch or down on the dock, in the summery comfort of rattan and wicker.

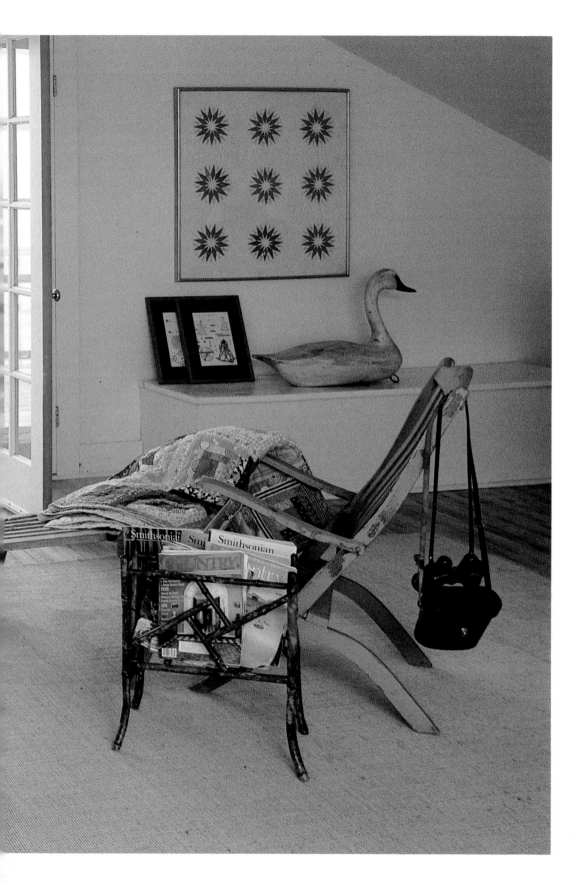

With a commanding view of the bay, the all-purpose family room on the second floor displays a few well-chosen nautical objects—a working model of a schooner, a quilt top, patterned after a mariner's compass, dating from 1850, and a deck chair from the era of the ocean liner.

ABOVE AND RIGHT: Rattan
and wicker furniture offer views
from a wraparound porch with
rough-hewn arches. An old croquet set on wheels and a string
hammock offer alternatives for
weekend afternoons.

Thomas K. Woodard
and Blanche Greenstein

BECAUSE ITS FAÇADE IS IMPECCABLE IN ITS FED-
eral details, this 1780 house is listed in the National Register of Historic Places. The Ashley
House was saved from the wrecking ball in
Fall River, Massachusetts, by Weatherhill Restoration, a group of skilled
preservationists, then moved in some 2,000 parts to a new location in
New York. Reassembled with the zeal and craftsman-
ship of a traditional barn raising, the house now ◣ *Long Island*
stands in its former glory, enriching a modern generation with the character and charm of a classic American building style.

"We ended up with a house that had every modern convenience and the
soul of an antique," says Thomas K. Woodard. The historic house of one
of Fall River's founding families was acquired piecemeal and reassembled,

but Tom Woodard and Blanche Greenstein, partners in a Manhattan quilt and antiques business, discovered that it was possible not only to put Humpty Dumpty back together again, but also to install new wiring, plumbing, and proper insulation at the same time.

The result is a house replete with authentic architectural detail, containing folk art, painted farm furniture, quilts, hooked rugs, and an easygoing space "where we could cook and friends could sit by the fire," says Blanche. "I like folksy things and furniture that is pure, simple, and clean. And I don't mind mixing the old with the new."

The parlor fireplace is as imposing in the Federal style, conveying formality and symmetry, as is the front entry with its crown and elliptical fanlight. In the keeping room at the back of the house, a fireplace built from bricks saved from the original structure offers a more countrified version of the hearth.

This room, though a new addition, incorporates recycled chestnut floorboards, posts and beams, and feathered-edged sheathing for wall paneling—all from the original 18th-century house. A wall of French doors adds plenty of light to this versatile space, evocative of the past, which leads to a modern kitchen and porch.

Folk art, painted buckets, Indian baskets, and jasper earthenware also give expression to the crafts of another time, in a house saved from extinction by history-minded carpenters of today.

OPPOSITE PAGE: In keeping with the formality of the parlor, a tone set by the exquisitely carved mantelpiece, the floor was painted and marbleized in a classic diamond pattern. Period reproduction furniture shares the space with such early-19th-century pieces as the English marquetry candlestand. ABOVE: An authentic Federal staircase, with its original cherry handrail, boldly turned balusters, and carved brackets, shines in the reflected glory of an Early American mirror.

RIGHT: **An antique basket with dried roses serves as a centerpiece on a Pennsylvania hutch table.**
BELOW: **A rabbit warren of tiny rooms in a rear wing gives way to an open space flooded with light. Original ceiling beams and chest-nut floorboards preserve the period feeling.**
OPPOSITE PAGE: **An old wooden sundial and an anonymous por-trait,** *Young Girl in a Blue Dress,* **dated 1835, breathe timeless beauty into the dining room.**

ABOVE: In the keeping
room, a decorative
glass window and an
elliptical door pediment
provide contrasting
architectural elements
from the mid-19th
century. The fireplace
wall still retains its
original feather-edged
wood paneling.

OPPOSITE PAGE:
Authentic colors of the
period are found in the
hall, from the earthy
reds of a New England
wall cupboard and a
redware lamp to the
bleached hues of a
country cabinet, work
stool, storage box, and
wood pitcher.

ABOVE AND BELOW
LEFT: Rare quilts and
folk art add a precious
sense of heritage to
modernized bedrooms.
The crib quilt on the
wall, made for a baby
named Louisa, dates
from 1851. The pattern
of the quilt on the
window seat is called
Drunkard's Path.
OPPOSITE PAGE:
Upon a timeworn
dough box, traditional
adversaries strike a
peaceful pose in their
Sunday best. The
stuffed animals are
newly made, but out-
fitted in antique ging-
hams and prints.

AMERICAN COUNTRY STYLE REACHES HEIGHTS OF ELEGANCE in homes reflecting a taste for luxury and romance, just as, historically, house design became more refined, as exemplified in Georgian architecture, and households became more style conscious, when the United States began to prosper as a nation. People turned to Philadelphia, Boston, Newport, and New York, thriving centers of furniture and cabinet making, as well *Romantic* as to Great Britain and "the Continent," to outfit themselves and their homes with the latest fashions. The fancy curves and curls of Chippendale and the crisp carvings of Sheraton and Hepplewhite contrasted markedly with the homemade plainness of ladder-back chairs and harvest tables. Rich Redouté botanicals replaced homely samplers on the walls. The houses come by their air of elegance in different ways, but each of them attests to the creativity of the people who live in them and the versatility of their  singular collections.

Bruce and Andrea Dern

Legendary movie director Frank Capra would have approved of the romantic splendor now encompassing the Malibu, California, beach house where he once lived. The warmhearted values of classic Capra films, such as *It Happened One Night* and *It's a Wonderful Life,* are present in gardens where handmade birdhouses and antique roses mingle in near-wild profusion. No harsh "colorization" spoils the effect: flowers are grown for their ◥ *Malibu, California* fragrances and their delicate shades of blue, pink, cream, lilac, and other pastels. In keeping with the unexpected rambling cottage garden, the house too is one delightful surprise after another, full of an artist's love of the natural world and the small treasures of domesticity she has passionately collected over the years.

90

Heirloom rose varieties selected for their fragrance and pastel shades flourish in a romantic seaside garden paved with old bricks and bordered by a picket fence with a built-in windshield.

"My mother's name is Violet Rose and I know I got my love of gardening from her," says Andrea Dern, who grew up on a North Dakota ranch. "As kids, my brother and I grew our own vegetables, and Mother would let us plant moss roses all over the place."

When Andrea and her husband, the actor Bruce Dern, first moved into their Malibu bungalow years ago, she knew exactly what to do with the "big sandpile with a single yucca tree" on the beach side of the house.

Planting all the trees, shrubs, vines, and flowers herself, Andrea transformed a bare California dune into a garden of Victorian delights, then surrounded it with a white picket fence of her own design, complete with glass panels to protect her old-fashioned flowers from wind and spray.

"It's a true cottage garden," says Andrea. "I planted it ramble-scramble right up to the doors. I like everything overgrown, so it looks like a secret garden that hasn't been tended for a long time." She adds with a laugh, "Bruce is just the opposite. He likes the garden best in February, when everything's been pruned back to the nubs!"

A painter and collector as well as gardener, Andrea drew on her artistic vision in her renovation of the 1929 dwelling. Working with an architect, she brought an existing freestanding teahouse into the plan of the main house and revived the tradition of high tea to celebrate the airy new structure. Upstairs, she introduced a happy version of the greenhouse effect, designing a combination potting shed/Jacuzzi for one corner of her studio.

Wanting "a cottagy look," she set out her collections of old watering cans, doorstops, and birdhouses of her own making —a skill she learned from her father. She

Pyramidal skylights, a pine floor painted in a checkerboard pattern, and a multitude of windows add the character of an English cottage to a renovated teahouse overlooking the Pacific. A magnet for visitors, the room is filled with old country furniture in Andrea's favorite color and friendly American collectibles like birdhouses and a 3-foot-high architectural model with a tin roof.

SHORE LOTS

Romantic motifs of the Victorian garden are captured in a comfortable nook where humble watering cans assemble in artful dignity. Beneath a peg rack laden with horticultural implements stands the first model Andrea collected—an intriguing farmhouse, all its windows shuttered closed.

LEFT: Flowers both fresh and re-produced, on fabric and crochet, add elegance to an old vineyard table rebuilt to capture California's storied natural resource. A house model complete with fence was the home of the family cats when they were kittens.

ABOVE: Iron doorstops, idle art-work of housewives of the early 1900s, show the way upstairs beneath a decorative beveled-glass window.

OPPOSITE PAGE: Everything comes up roses on the Victorian wicker buffet in the studio.

ABOVE RIGHT: A wall inset with mirrors allows back-porch views of two contrasting home styles of the past. The antique English stand for muffins and scones serves at tea parties of today.

RIGHT: The parlor has the stamp of English country comforts with a horticultural theme. The still life over the mantel was painted by American artist J. W. Orthe in the 1940s.

ABOVE: In the bedroom aerie, the antique crocheted bedcover from England sports a border of birds. Flourishes on floor and cupboard are the work of Andrea Dern.
LEFT: Andrea paints the old-fashioned glories of her own garden in a naive style.
OPPOSITE PAGE: A cottage garden of earthly delights, a rare sight in California, beckons visitors through French doors surmounted by an opalescent medallion in the transom.

also contributed her own deft stenciling, needlework, and "funky little flower paintings" to bring the casual elegance of the flower garden into the house.

Garden and home flow together so naturally that it is clear Andrea has put her heart into it all. And her unfailing gifts can also be seen in her collection of miniature farmhouses, lighthouses, cottages, mansions, and churches. "They were built as a novelty by grandfather for grandchild," says Andrea, explaining their origin. "It might have been someone with time on his hands who just wanted to make a tiny likeness of the family home."

When Bruce is on location for a new film, Andrea travels with him, enjoying the chance to scout new areas and perhaps come upon another watering can or "anything connected with the garden. I grew up in a farm," she notes, "and I think you like what you grew up with."

The garden overflows with delphiniums, climbing roses and jasmine, and dozens of other varieties of flowering perennials.

Eugenie Voorhees

IN AN OLD SAILING VILLAGE OVERLOOKING NANtucket Harbor, a small but handsome shingle-style house built in 1757 has regained its original dignity thanks to a renovation that stripped the building of inauthentic details, such as exterior shutters and window boxes, imposed over the years. Inside, rooms were "peeled like an onion" to reveal the natural beauty ◣ *Nantucket* of paneled walls, mottled doors, and pine floors. True to the simple aesthetic of the Quakers, who were among the island's first settlers, the house is minimally furnished—though not without the owner's welcome stamp of unorthodoxy—its walls bare, its essence captured in the purity and play of space and light, unusual features in a traditional home.

"We just edited the house back to the way it should have been," says Eugenie Voorhees of her renovation, with distinguished American architect Hugh Newell Jacobsen. Seven generations of islanders had lived in the small, well-proportioned house, and periods of neglect had taken their toll.

The architect first oriented the floor plan to the quiet side of the house, away from the commercial bustle of Orange Street, one of the most authentic 18th-century neighborhoods in America. Then, floors, walls, woodwork, and old pine doors were scraped down until their seasoned character was revealed. "Underneath everything were the colors of the original milk paint bonding to the wood," Jacobsen relates.

When I first walked up to this house in what I think of as the ultimate New England town, I could only imagine an interior chockablock with American antiques. Much to my surprise and delight, I found myself in rooms devoid of any period decoration. The plain backgrounds and stripped woodwork were the focal points rather than the objects within.

Having spent summers on Nantucket all her life, Eugenie had decided she wanted a simple house closer to the traditions of the earliest settlers. "They didn't run out and buy yards of chintz and have a bunch of furniture," she says.

Although spare in concept, the house is comfortable, warmed by the play of natural light that filters through windows outfitted with shutters—not the 18th-century kind, but simple ones obtained from Sears. So restrained are the rooms in this house that some appreciative visitors have asked, "When will you be finished?" Says Eugenie, "I just tell them, 'Oh, when I get around to it.' "

Pickled pine floors and milk-painted wainscoting, dating from 200 years ago, mark the master bedroom with tradition, while an imported chaise longue adds modern comfort.

ABOVE: Instead of pictures, a composition of rectangular panels and roll molding, authentic to the 18th century, adds beauty to the fireplace wall and conceals essential doorways and cabinets. A balsa model of a Rainbow-class sailboat and the mohair throw are examples of island craftsmanship. LEFT: On a slab of polished Brazilian granite in the living room, a Shaker miniature rocks to its own tune. An ardent reader's collection of books creates a wall of color and lively graphics in the otherwise austere setting.

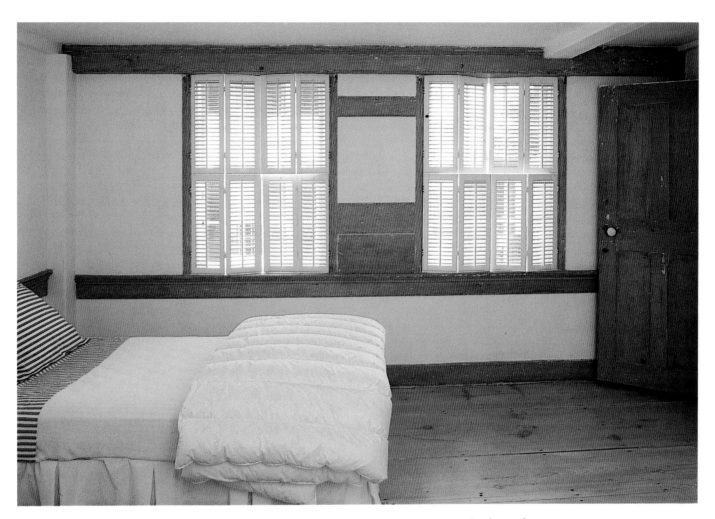

ABOVE: As throughout the house, the guest bedroom draws on the bare bones of the venerable dwelling for its unadorned beauty.
OPPOSITE PAGE: Stripped down to its essentials, the bathroom makes use of a 19th-century blanket rack and a Shaker stool instead of hardware.

A narrow English pine farmhouse table and a set of steel park chairs from Toulouse, France, "much more comfortable than they look," are all that's needed for a gathering centered on friends and food.

Patrick and Elizabeth Gerschel

THE DREAMY ELEGANCE OF A CLASSIC AMERICAN shingled house, dating from the first decade of the 19th century, stems as much from the present owner's infatuation with flowers, especially the rose, as it does from the high aspirations of the original builder, Edward Mulford, a prosperous landowner and heir of the West Indies shipping trade. The first owner provided ◢ *New York State* his family's dwelling with such stylish Georgian details as the crowned and pilastered front door; the woman who lives here now gave the house a setting of gardens, ensuring that her beloved flowers would breathe romance, delicacy, and life into every room inside. A classic 18th-century gardening treatise, *American Gardens* by Ann Leighton, gave Elizabeth Gerschel her inspiration for creating a new Colonial

116

garden for her country house in New York State. Today, the backyard teems with colorful heirloom varieties of herbs and flowers and, a lifelong botanical favorite of her own, the delicate hues of old-fashioned roses like Betty Pryor, Iceberg, and New Dawn.

Elizabeth, who was my next-door neighbor when I first moved to the country, acquired her house as a stunningly unexpected wedding present from her husband, Patrick. By this time it had passed through many generations of families of merchants and ship captains and was beginning to look less than seaworthy. Elizabeth accomplished a sensitive and livable restoration, even saving three rustic outbuildings for charming contemporary use around pool and garden.

"The house makes me feel the history of the area and the whole country. We've made some adaptations and added modern touches," she says, "but the formal captain's house has set the style to follow."

Thus, Elizabeth made sure the "modern" flooring, laid over the original wide-plank pumpkin-pine floor throughout the house, was removed so that the original surfaces could be sanded and waxed back to their original "creaky and uneven" beauty.

Thanks to its 8-foot ceilings and generous windows, the house is incredibly airy and light. "We keep the windows and doors open to the outside for as long as possible, which is why our brass keeps turning yellow."

Even at night the lighting has a special quality. Because they use candlelight everywhere, "everything kind of glows—the wood, the gilt frames, everything," she says, adding, "When the fire is lit and the candles are going, it's hard to believe how soft and pretty the light can be."

ABOVE: **This rustic solarium, used as a tearoom from which to enjoy views of the garden, was once a chicken coop.**
OPPOSITE PAGE: **Brick-red Eyepaint roses parade in front of the pool house, formerly a horse barn; a grape arbor cools the brick-patio porch.**

Twelve-over-twelve windows and
a four-light transom in the door,
original to the house, provide a
classic Georgian backdrop for the
vintage Bar Harbor wicker and
new Doric columns on the porch.

A spade-top picket fence, covered with delicate-hued New Dawn roses, holds pool and yard in formal embrace.

LEFT: **A tilt-top tea table holds a riot of New Dawn and White Dawn roses in a stoneware milk jug and salt-glaze creamers.**
RIGHT: **An 18th-century parlor combines the new owner's love of flowers with appurtenances authentic to the time, including a gilt English girandole mirror, a built-in cupboard of English creamware, and an American candlestand. Ladies once protected their wax-based cosmetics with heat shields, on top of the mantel.**

OPPOSITE PAGE: **The dining room basks in a hundred points of candlelight. Connecticut-made satinwood chairs, with shield backs and swag-tacked seats, address a table setting crowned with a triple scoop of crabapple blossoms in creamware. The over-the-mantel mirror comes with its own candelabrum.**

RIGHT: **Five 18th-century brass candlesticks from England illumine a portrait of eight-year-old Adelaide Pierce, painted in 1835 by American artist Alexander C. McLean.**

ABOVE: By the old kitchen hearth, an 18th-century English table made with versatile gate legs stands with two variants on the Windsor chair.
RIGHT: Chintz in the sitting room celebrates the beauty of hydrangeas, a prolific local bloomer. An 18th-century wheel-back chair, painted red and decorated with flowers, pays heed to the garden.
OPPOSITE PAGE: Spongeware, common on the domestic scene all along the Eastern Seaboard in the 18th century, now forms a colorful collection in the corner cupboard.

LEFT: The pencil-post pine bed in the guest bedroom is outfitted with an 18th-century wedding trousseau of crocheted tester, pillow shams, and quilt. The stained Hepplewhite night table and white painted trunk also date from that period.
OPPOSITE PAGE: Patterns of an old quilt, striped valance, and the wing chair and curtains mix agreeably in the master bedroom. On the table is the Bible, bound in ivory, that four generations of women have carried on their wedding day.

A Historic Saltbox House

ON CAPE COD, A CLASSIC FIVE-BAY saltbox house with center chimney, constructed in about 1740 for the Bourne family, epitomizes the understated elegance of the Georgian building style. Although only a stone's throw from town, the house sits with majestic reserve on four rolling acres planted by an earlier owner, a horticulturist, with beautiful trees, including chestnuts, English and American elms, cop- ◣ *Cape Cod* per beeches, ginkgos, and lilac trees. Inside, thanks to the present owners, collectors devoted to their historic home, the original rooms of the house possess the textures, colors, and refinement characteristic of early America's emerging middle class.

If I had to cast a movie about the life of the quintessential antiques dealer, I would give the starring roles to the couple who live here, two

collectors who never weary of the thrill of hunting for the very best in authentic American antiques. Ten years ago, when I first visited the organized clutter of their shop on Nantucket, I marveled at both the quality and quantity of their finds, with what seemed like hundreds of firkins in near pristine condition in one room, an equal number of impeccable old baskets in the next, and so on through the store.

The couple bring the same sharp eye and warm appreciation for the past to their historic but ever-changing home on Cape Cod. "Our house is like a French stew," says the husband. "We're always putting things in and taking them out."

The result is a surprising combination of patterns and colors, painted and polished surfaces, and intriguing objects in every room. Unlike homes with a "sprayed-on" period look, the rooms in this house haven't been set up just for the initial impact, but instead they invite friends to linger and enjoy, with antiques and collections filling every corner.

The pair are purist in their approach to collecting, insisting on "the best of the best," but they don't take their antiques so seriously that they fail to get pleasure from them. "An elderly woman told me once," his wife recalls, " 'Take care of your antiques, and they will take care of you.' "

The effort of the hunt and the investment has repaid them with a home that is so much fun to live in, they never can make up their minds in which room they want to settle for an evening—or even where to sit. A sociable couple, they love to cook and entertain, and they've filled their house with chairs of every description. "In the 18th century," he points out, "the inventories of family estates show that chairs were often the most numerous of a person's possessions."

Elegance without fussiness, hallmark of the well-to-do Georgian home, is suggested by this "great room," which began life as a humble kitchen. The brick hearth with its narrow pine mantel, the dark-stained pine-sheathed wall, and most of the natural pine beams, now oxidized with age, are original to the house. The English and tin-glazed Delft earthenware patterns over the fireplace reflect Chinese Export porcelain.

LEFT: The formal symmetry of the dining room evokes an 18th-century household of substance, its fortune perhaps linked to trading vessels like the clipper ship in the painting by Elisha Taylor Baker. Silver from the era, including a revolving Sheffield service for keeping food warm, and the Chinese Export temple jars, punch bowl, and tureen also hint of profitable routes on the high seas.

ABOVE: A stately corner cupboard, made in Pennsylvania in 1790, sparkles with early English and American ceramics and silver spoons crafted on Nantucket as early as 1760.
LEFT: An 1835 oil portrait of Captain John Pease and a mahogany clock made on Cape Cod circa 1815 both command respect in the hallway to the rear of house. Leather fire buckets were painted with the owner's name to ensure their return following a town emergency.

In the kitchen cupboard, a collection of Canton porcelain china dating from the early 19th century provides a visual rhapsody in blue and white.

ABOVE: A corner of
the kitchen has a mar-
ble-top center island,
over which hang mar-
ket baskets from early
Nantucket lightships.
The tartan plaid floor
was painted in twelve
separate stages.

RIGHT: Pantry firkins from Nantucket, a gilded copper weathervane, circa 1870, in the form of a
codfish, and the 1915 portrait of
Provincetown Neptune holding his
cod catch offer a tribute to the
Cape's maritime heritage.

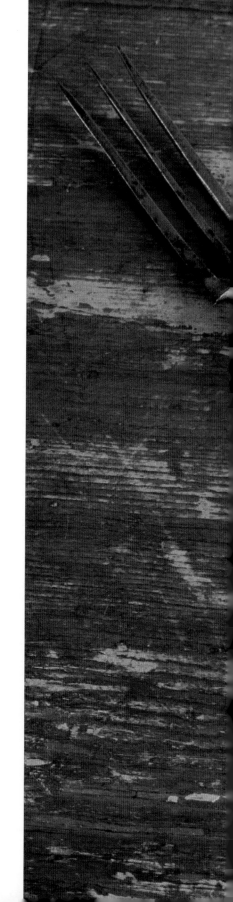

As the American frontier pushed westward on the heels of homesteaders, ranchers, sheepherders, and other settlers, utilitarian needs of day-to-day survival dictated home style on the farm and in the wilderness. American Country in its most rustic form is represented by houses in which all elements, from stone fireplaces to split-rail fences and peeled-log walls, were built and set in place by the homeowner, his family, and his neighbors. Builders, cabinetmakers, and *Rustic* other craftsmen culled the raw materials for their trades from their surroundings, yielding a rich and varied regionalism. Hand-fashioned tools, implements, and furniture were built to last, and to serve practical, not frivolous, purposes. Functionality has given them primitive beauty. These objects mean much to us today because they bear the unmistakable stamp of a human hand. Even when modern comforts are introduced into a rustic dwelling, the legacy of frontier days remains intact.

A Former
Sheepherder's Cottage

Bounded by the Atlantic Ocean and pastures, a former sheepherder's cottage in East Hampton, built in the 1700s, today embodies the feeling of its time without sacrificing comfort. The owner's collection of scrimshaw and whalebone remnants pays homage to the seafaring tradition of the era; well-worn firehouse Windsor chairs and a well-used trestle table invite visitors to relax in a genu-

◥ *East Hampton, Long Island*

inely rustic setting. In an ingenious piece of restoration, insulation was added to exterior walls so that the rugged lines of the chestnut shell of the house remain exposed. Combined, these unpretentious elements create what the owner describes as her "emotional home," a retreat for simple pursuits and lasting pleasures.

A Scottish-pine lambing chair from the 19th century reminds of the shepherd who first lived in the cottage; the eeling spear, a sheet-metal ship from a weathervane, and a seaman's chest reflect a nautical tradition. A central chimney fireplace, painted white to highlight its rugged contours, dominates the room.

When this tiny, centuries-old farm cottage was discovered by its present owners, it was riddled with more than 100 phone jacks—incongruously, the dwelling had been used as the office for a modern telephone answering service. The professional couple who now own the cottage enlisted the help of designer Robert K. Lewis, a specialist in 18th-century architecture, to turn it into a comfortable weekend residence for their family.

An extensive renovation produced livable quarters and yet returned the dwelling to its rustic traditions. "There were very few original elements to work with," explains Lewis, "since most of the floors and walls had been removed or replaced."

The designer made the central brick chimney, with its warm and hospitable character, the heart of the the main room. The pickled and bleached oak floors and the blue-painted stair boards, recycled to clad a kitchen work counter, add a distinctive charm.

I have long admired Robert's eye for detail and when we happen to be on the antiques trail at the same time, I am always curious to know what treasures he has unearthed. In this house, the eeling spear over the mantel not only stands out in relief against the chimney, but also adds a meaningful regional footnote.

Robert draws on the natural world of earth, stone, and wood for his palette of puttylike colors, but he is not such a rigid purist that he would make you sit on a rock. For the upholstered seating in the cottage, he chose a practical jute-colored linen, and filled it with enough goose down to ensure comfort fit for a king—or queen. As the lady of the house likes to tell Robert, appreciatively, over the phone whenever she comes out, "I just want to say that we're here and we love it."

LEFT: The putty blue of a work counter clad in boards recycled from the staircase of another old house nearly matches the hue of agateware, made for the American trade in the 1800s, on a steel plate stand of the same vintage.

RIGHT: A bedroom created out of a tiny back porch has a new pine floor, bleached and pickled, and a four-poster finished to match. The 19th-century finery on the bed includes a Marseilles spread with a woven jacquard pattern and elaborately detailed pillow slips made in Pennsylvania, probably as part of an Early American bridal trousseau.

Ryan Carey
and Mac McLean

A SCULPTOR'S CRAFT, COMBINING found materials with "eggshell" plaster to produce unique works of art, and an artist's eye, finding treasures where others only notice trash, are the dominating influences in a rustic California Spanish house, located in the center of ultra-urban Los Angeles. Here, the sense of nature is tempered by a sense of history: textures evoking the larger-than-life West of Old California, a colorful collection of 1930s pottery from ◤ *Los Angeles* south of the border, and the exclusion of any of the appurtenances of the technological world. The swap meet is California's version of the flea market, a huge parking-lot bazaar where one pack rat's junk is another's prized find. I especially enjoy going to swap meets with constructivist sculptor Ryan Carey and his business manager, Mac McLean, because it's

fun to watch them make so many unexpected discoveries. And I get the same visual rewards when I visit their 1932 California Spanish house, its small rooms brimming with collections so tactile you want to handle them all.

Two blocks from the original Disney Studios in the Griffith Park area of Los Angeles, the house offers views of both the Pacific and the mountains, but what's inside is even more interesting. There are fine examples of Ryan's own work, vessels of "eggshell plaster"—often incorporating found materials of old wood, leather, feathers, beads, bones, stones, and shells. And there are the collections the two have amassed separately and together: earthy Bauer pottery of the 1930s, old Indian baskets, painted terra-cotta objects made in Mexico for the American market in the 1920s and 1930s, and colorful dishes from a United Nations of countries.

To accommodate these treasures, the pair undertook to restore the house to its original 1920s folk beauty. First ripping out the ersatz Spanish trim that had been added along the way, they split and mitered old logs to create new window moldings and doorjambs. Painting, then hand-stripping, they laboriously antiqued all the wood surfaces in the house. Inspired by a detail in a Frank Lloyd Wright house, they built shelves at just below ceiling height for both storage and display.

"I especially love the old Mexican things," says Ryan. "Each one looks as if it took only a few minutes to make, but I know if I tried to draw a tree on the side of a pot in as few strokes as they did, it would probably look like a lollipop."

Mac is fascinated by the stories behind the ordinary objects used in daily life: "I wish I could find out where each thing came from, what it was for, how it was made."

OPPOSITE PAGE:
Mexican, English, and
Chinese pottery fills
every available space in
the breakfast nook,
including the recycled
butcher's meat hook by
the window. The hand-
painted Art Deco light
fixture was made in
Mexico. A bronze table
lamp of the California
craftsman school dates
from the same period.
LEFT: An English-style
fireplace was replaced
with a hearth hand-
fashioned from local
river rock to suggest
the adobe architecture
of early California. A
stucco mantel holds a
Mexican charger and
jars from the 1930s.
Placating the Spirit is
the name of the found
terra-cotta pot Ryan
Carey transformed
with wood, rawhide,
and iron.

153

LEFT: A gas stove made in Milwaukee in 1925 finds its niche in a kitchen stacked with Bauer ring-pattern pottery and a mixed brood of Mexican and California "chicken ware." The square-handled casserole with its quaint painted country scene is an exemplary work from south of the border.
RIGHT: A kitchen houses a 1930s china cupboard displaying an array of pottery from Mexico, California, Japan, and Europe. Fine examples of Pacific drip ware, as well as two antique spatterware bowls from France, rest on the counter.

RIGHT: On a scarred table rescued from the Mojave Desert, Ryan Carey's *Tribute to Georgia* binds an old Mexican terra-cotta vessel, newly polychromed, to the jawbone of a cow in a tribute to the Southwest painter Georgia O'Keeffe. The Navajo Yei doll figures on the wall were carved by Navajo Emmett Lee. The antique mesquite doors originally graced a Mexican Colonial hacienda. LEFT: In a narrow stairwell, skulls bleached on the open range contrast with colorful "Ali Baba" jars made by Bauer.

Navajo blankets and a well-used washstand give a rustic feeling to the master bedroom.

Joel Schumacher

A BUILDING THAT ONCE STABLED RUDOLPH Valentino's Arabian horses has been transformed into a rustic homestead with exotic touches the romantic matinee idol would have appreciated. The exterior, revived to resemble "what a visitor arriving on horseback would have seen in 1925," boasts a profusion of bougainvillea, agave, jasmine, and other native California ◣ *Southern California* vegetation. Inside, the rooms adhere to their original simple layout, but thanks to the discerning eye of an unconventional collector, they are literally piled high with Native American blankets and rugs and other colorful relics of Southwestern culture. The owner's playful spirit and powerful imagination have combined to produce a livable fantasy worthy of its Old Hollywood predecessors.

The southern California home of Joel Schumacher offers a rich tapestry of texture and complexity. When I first stopped by, I was impressed with his ability to bring color and pattern into the house layer by layer. A native New Yorker who worked his way through art school by dressing the store windows in Henri Bendel, Joel is now a successful film director and screenwriter who applies his eye for visual effect to both his work and home.

He first started collecting Indian rugs and blankets when he came to California in 1971. "I'd never seen anything like them before," he recalls, adding, "I'm probably a foolish collector, because I respond only to what appeals to me emotionally. I've never bought anything because it had an investment value."

The cleaned-up, rustic look of the small, airy rooms in his house is instantly appealing. A less striking but equally charming element is Joel's talent for comic relief—a Pee Wee Herman doll next to a 17th-century oil painting, or the cylinder from an old jet plane as a coffee table.

Joel claims ignorance about the fine points of home design—"I don't know a Chippendale from a Hepplewhite"—but when he first moved into his house he embarked on a sensitive renovation of both dwelling and grounds. He restored the stucco walls, added terra-cotta tile floors, and sought out doors and gates from the Southwest desert to match the period in the 1920s when the house was built.

"Out here, you often see houses trying to be English Tudors or French chateaus or Italian discotheques," says Joel. "I wanted a house that would be comfortable for my friends and me and yet stay true to the California of its era."

ABOVE: *The Crucifixion,* painted in 1984 by Dominic Cretera, offers a dramatic modern view of an ancient theme, while an African basket, used to hold kindling, and the fragment of a Corinthian wood column, made in Mexico, add their own texture to the tapestry of the room.

OPPOSITE PAGE: An Indian chief's striped blanket and a pair of carved wood columns from an 1800s Mexican church lead the way to the dining room.

A chair with the formality of a throne, but covered in unpedigreed cowhide, presides over one man's collection of Native American rugs and blankets, a riot of bold patterns in the living room.

ABOVE: Portraits of Señor and Señora Andreas Pico, early Mexican settlers who made good as California ranchers, occupy the place of honor at the head of the bed; painted metal trunks, humble luggage of the Old West, take their place at the foot.

RIGHT: The pencil-post bed, layered with serapes and Navajo blankets, was built by a local craftsman.

OPPOSITE PAGE: A Chinese shipping crate and an old door from Santa Fe, treated as a shelf, are replete with rusticated wares, including an African work basket.

A wooden portal from a Santa Fe hacienda and a few serape-draped chaise longues are all that's needed to transport this poolside setting to Old Mexico.

Peter and Lynda Guber

HIGH IN THE ROCKY MOUNTAINS outside Aspen, Colorado, Hollywood film producer, and now Chairman of the Board of Columbia Pictures, Peter Guber and wife Lynda have created a dramatic family retreat that has the look and feel of a grand Western lodge. Private, yet not isolated, the 100-acre site affords a spectacular wide-screen panorama on all sides, including views of White River National Forest. The Gubers and their daughters,

Aspen, Colorado

Jodi and Elizabeth, take advantage of the surroundings by frequent outings right from their property on skis, snowmobile, and horseback. Upon their return, the house welcomes them with its expanses of wood, cozy fireplaces, and colorful reminders of the cowboys and Native Americans who first tamed this beautiful wilderness.

170

"You know, we always dreamed of building our own log cabin," says Lynda Guber in describing the more than 10,000-square-foot family compound she and husband Peter have built in the Colorado Rockies. "I guess you could say we just got carried away."

Although the scale of their fantasy home, which they have given the appropriately cinematic name "Mandalay," is large, with soaring cathedral ceilings and six generous guest suites, the atmosphere of the interiors is inviting and intimate. Navajo rugs, animal skins, natural wood surfaces, stylish yet comfortable seating, and a hearth in almost every room all combine to infuse the house with a hospitable, welcoming spirit. The numerous photos scattered throughout are accorded the same place of honor as the couple's remarkable collection of the photographic prints of Edward S. Curtis, the pioneering chronicler of Native American life.

"We wanted the house to have a place for everyone to gather," explains Lynda. "When we had our 80-foot yacht, everybody always ended up in our room when we went sailing. We decided to design the house with plenty of space for people to get together, but also with their own private retreats. That's how the bedroom suites, each with its own fireplace, bath, and entertainment system, came about."

With movies like *Flashdance, Rain Man,* and *Batman* to his credit, Peter Guber knows what it takes to produce a hit, but when it came to Mandalay, it was tranquility, not spectacle, that he was after. "Here the full range of one's imagination can be employed and no one will comment," he says.

ABOVE: The rugged spirit of the region is conveyed in a fireplace made from local river rock, a ceiling covered with *latillas* in the Southwestern adobe tradition, and a collection of century-old Navajo rugs.

OPPOSITE PAGE: Carved from swamp cypress by Aspen sculptor Eddie Running Wolf, the double doors usher visitors into a world indelibly stamped with the Western wilderness.

LEFT: Pine logs from Montana lend their massive strength to a dining room graced with a pair of saguaro cacti and a chandelier made of moose antlers.
OPPOSITE PAGE: Furniture in the rustic "Home on the Range" tradition of Thomas Molesworth occupies the horse barn, the family's recreational outpost. Saddle mounts are covered with Native American weavings.

Uprooted tree trunks have been skillfully used to reinterpret the conventional four-poster as a suitable bed for the Wild West. The ceiling beam is decorated in a Native American motif borrowed from a favorite lodge in Yosemite National Park.

ABOVE: A modern bathroom retains the ambience of the frontier with appurtenances like the double vanity, converted from a venerable farmhouse worktable.

RIGHT: A bleached skull and old Pendleton blankets for the Indian trade are reminders of range life, as authentic as the river rock of the fireplace with its water-worn contours.

ABOVE: In the master suite, a massive lodgepole pine bed receives its warmth from Navajo blankets and an otterskin throw. Pillows are covered with pony hide, as are the chair and ottoman. Over the fireplace is a relic of butterfly collecting—an early stun gun that shot sand charges.

OPPOSITE PAGE: The river-rock bath is a soothing natural retreat for the cleansing of body and spirit, intimate yet open to the light.

Michael and Eleanore Kennedy

IN A SEASIDE HOUSE BUILT FOR A DISTINGUISHED theologian in 1879, a spare beauty almost spiritual in nature has been brought back to life through a loving and sensitive restoration. Eleanore Kennedy preserved the original integrity of the dwelling, after it fell into disrepair, by taking her cues from the home's natural setting and designing with restraint rather than embellishment.

◥ *Long Island*

In transforming old riding tack, found in the barn, into a sculpture for one corner of the house, or bringing together a gift from a Texas friend with gifts from the sea to make a mantelpiece "as spare and bare" as the house itself, she has demonstrated how ordinary objects can be deployed with the decorative force of rare antiques.

Overlooking the sand dunes of Long Island's south shore, Kilkare

House was built for Jonathan Edwards, a preacher and theologian, in 1879, complete with wide porches and nine fireplaces. If the prevailing taste of the times, and of the original owner, was Victorian, the bias of the construction crew, made up of accomplished local ship and dock builders, was distinctly nautical.

It is the deft craftsmanship of those artisans, seen in such details as flying buttress–like arches on the front porch, the soaring staircase from the main room to the second-floor landing, the handsome built-in cupboards and dressers in many of the rooms, and the one-of-a-kind ceilings —each the product of a gifted carpenter's kaleidoscopic vision—that gives this dwelling its lasting beauty.

When Eleanore and Michael Kennedy acquired the property fifteen years ago, the house had fallen into disrepair, but Eleanore was quick to recognize its wonderful architectural features as well as to sense the mystique of its privileged location, "right at a point where air, water, and land meet," she explains. "I wanted our design for the restoration to preserve the integrity of that joining."

In bringing the house back to life, she stressed clean, uncluttered lines, brightness, clarity, "and most of all honesty." I especially like the way the beauty of the wood plays off the white of the ceilings and walls throughout the house.

"Nature and the man I love inspired me," says Eleanore of her efforts to rejuvenate Kilkare House. In some ways it was the fulfillment of a childhood fantasy. "When I was very small," she recalls, "I would dream of having a beautiful house by the sea, a man who loved me, and a rocking chair," adding, "That's why, when the man and I found this house, I knew I needed to have some rockers."

Drawing its light and color from the natural world, the uncluttered sitting room with its bare pumpkin-pine floors, canvas-covered window seat, and old rattan chairs achieves an uncommon serenity. Low tables and ceramic-shell wall sconces are the owner's design.

RIGHT: Inside and out, the skill and traditions of the shipbuilders who crafted this house in 1879 are evident in such details as the Victorian stairwell leading to the ship's knee—a built-in bench on the landing where ladies had tea and watched the sailboats on Georgica Pond.
OPPOSITE PAGE: A wicker stroller from the early 1900s, once used for leisurely jaunts on the boardwalk in Atlantic City, still takes the salt air through sliding "pocket doors" of carved cherry and glass.

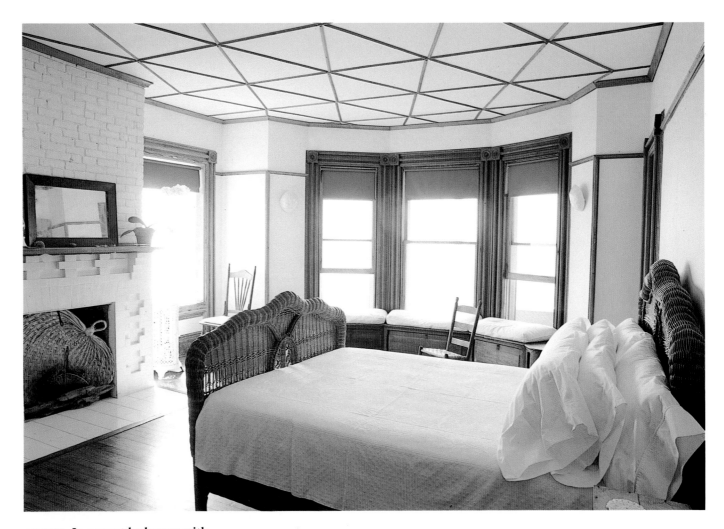

ABOVE: In a guest bedroom with a view, the fireplace, one of nine in the house, features a cross pattern in its brickwork. The ceiling of each room boasts its own wood-on-white geometric pattern.
RIGHT: Early plumbing came with its own backsplash and two legs to stand on. Clothes were hung on hooks in the shallow closet behind the primitive cherry door.
OPPOSITE PAGE: A Victorian rosewood dresser, made in San Francisco about 1900, features a beveled mirror and, to guard against spilled toiletries, a milk-glass top.

ABOVE: The master bedroom has a flame cherry four-poster bed that was found in the house all in pieces. Hanging lamps were installed with the advent of electricity after the turn of the century. LEFT: A bedroom wall is rich in texture because of the built-in cupboard and chest of drawers, a whimsically bricked fireplace, and oval frames, two with old photographs of Edwards women.

Buffy Birrittella

THE PEG RACK INSIDE A MOUNTAIN retreat in Sundance, Utah, speaks volumes for the rustic traditions of the pioneering homesteaders and ranchers who settled in these parts, just as an array of wildflowers, collected from the countryside, suggests the rich natural beauty of the surroundings. Out West, nothing is just for show: hand-tooled saddlebags, the fishing creel, and an Apache burden basket, its tassels tipped with silver, all had a utilitarian ◥ *Sundance, Utah* function. But just as the hat of every working cowboy reflects the personality of the individual wearing it, so too does this home reveal the strong personal style and character of its occupant. It's true to the West, and to the woman who has made it her own.

Buffy Birrittella fell in love with Sundance, Utah, the first time she

skied there fifteen years ago. Recently, when the community's most famous resident, Robert Redford, designed and built a group of "cottagy cabins," each in its own mountain fastness, she made her attachment to the area permanent.

The cabin, like its neighbors, reflects the actor/builder's well-known preservationist convictions with natural materials that follow the clean lines of Scandinavian architecture. Clad in cedar batten board on the outside, it has roughhewn spruce walls and flooring, pine doors, and fireplaces of chunky native sandstone. The rustic ambience provides an appropriate backdrop for tokens of Buffy's favorite pursuits, like horseback riding, fishing, and wildflower collecting, and for the vintage black-and-white photographs, horse miniatures, and the other artifacts she has collected with a knowing eye. Her home is as American as the annual Fourth of July celebration in the streets of nearby Provo.

"There's an integrity and honesty about the West, growing out of the struggle and hardships of the early settlers," says Buffy, "and it's managed to stay that way." Now senior vice president at Polo Ralph Lauren, Buffy has traveled all over the world, but Sundance is her healing escape from "the fast-paced existence."

For a decade Buffy has been collecting rugs and blankets made by Native Americans and by the old Pendleton and Beacon mills for the Indian trade, some of which have inspired items in Lauren's own successful home collections. Although she responds to the bright colors and "primitive boldness" in Navajo rugs, she is in awe of their craftsmanship. "The Navajo have always loved decoration," she notes, "because they see it as a way of revealing not just their wealth and status within the tribe, but their inner soul. They adhere

LEFT: A cabinet, made in New Mexico in the 1850s, suits a no-fuss kitchen equipped with locally made table and chairs of alderwood. New blue-and-white spongeware shares the shelf with cowboy-themed restaurant ware manufactured in Los Angeles in the 1940s. The wire stand once stored staples in a pantry.
ABOVE: A 1910 Navajo blanket, woven in a classic diamond pattern, sets off a pie safe with punched-tin panels, made in upstate New York in the 1860s, used to house the stereo.

ABOVE: A contemporary bedding collection by Ralph Lauren cohabits pleasingly with a 1920 fringed wool Pendleton blanket, used as a throw, the odd pillow covered with a Satillo serape remnant, and the Navajo rugs on floor, dating from 1910.

RIGHT: A heart-shaped mirror, made in the Adirondacks, is as much at home in the Wasatch range of the Rockies.

FAR RIGHT: An old child's chair with cowhide seat shares the fireside with a new chair upholstered in a design inspired by early Beacon Mills blankets, like the one draped over it. The iron-studded trunk belonged to "A.H.," a stagecoach passenger of yesteryear.

to the philosophy 'to walk in beauty.' "

The pioneers, too, put a lot of love, style, and personality into their handmade possessions, Buffy believes, and she collects and values those objects for the same reason. "That's why I still have the cole-slaw cutter my grandfather made."

The primitive beauty of our Western heritage isn't taken for granted by those who are closest to it. "Out here people hold on to their values *and* their possessions," she observes. "They don't throw things out as casually as we do back East. And the beautiful outdoors, with its awesome sense of space, gives people an intimation that there is something much bigger than themselves. You stay in touch with nature," Buffy concludes, "and that really keeps you in touch with yourself."

ABOVE: **An Early American hooked rug, made on the Pennsylvania/Ohio frontier from remnants, captures a horse's lively gait as "L.G." saw it.** LEFT: **A pre-1900 Pendleton blanket, its workmanship revealed front and back, and a pair of beaded cowgirl gloves, made by Plains Indians in 1890, remind of another age in the guest bedroom.**

LUCY M. LEWIS

A new room of roughhewn Englemann spruce bears witness to the Old West with photographs of Hopi women taken by Edward S. Curtis in the early 1900s, Pendleton and Beacon blankets from the same period, and two fine specimens from the owner's collection of folk art horses.

Derald and Janet Ruttenberg

A PRE-REVOLUTIONARY FARMHOUSE OF STONE and ivy, situated in one of the last undeveloped townships in Bucks County, Pennsylvania, is the weekend home of Janet and Derald Ruttenberg and their family. The "sincerity" of this venerable dwelling won over the Ruttenbergs when they first saw it twenty-two years ago, and it still reflects its heritage ◣ *Bucks County, Pennsylvania* in the way they have furnished and lived in it. But it also reflects the inimitable style of Janet Ruttenberg, an artist, as seen in the welcoming front porch, unconventionally painted in stripes and furnished with chairs made entirely of horseshoes and with a weather-beaten dry sink the color of faded denim. This juxtaposition of tradition and wit is what gives the house its wonderful sense of place.

202

When they relocated East from the Midwest some years ago, Janet and Derald Ruttenberg were first shown a house "that was all fixed up," Janet recalls with a shudder. "It was in perfect order down to the reproduction hardware. I hated it!"

As an afterthought, their realtor mentioned "a really untouched farmhouse" for sale in the town of Tinicum, so they went to look at it, in the rain. "It was authentic, sincere, like the farmhouses I grew up with in Iowa," Janet says. And, yes, it was untouched. "Some of the people who are still working on the house today knocked on the door shortly after we moved in and said, 'You're going to need help.'"

While her husband, a business executive who loves the outdoors, plunged into the task of reviving the neglected grounds, Janet traveled to the duPont museum in Winterthur, Delaware, to study the traditional uses and accoutrements of rooms in a house dating back to 1790. Then, drawing on her own creative talents, she added surprising details and played light against dark in the furnishings to make the home her own.

Then there is her own warm, welcoming personality. And if Janet's not there to greet me when I visit, her longtime assistant, Anna-Liisa Russell, an exuberant Finn, does the honors. Janet has expressed to me her appreciation for the countryside surrounding her home in every season: "the sweet, long-lasting spring, the heavy-scented lilies and softly glowing lightning bugs of summer, the wonderful colors of fall and its plenitude of migrating birds, and the stark, Breughelesque landscape of winter, thrillingly crossed by deer or wild turkey."

All of the richness of those observations can be seen in Janet Ruttenberg's home.

LEFT: The time-darkened 18th-century paneling of the doors flanking the fireplace (just one is visible here) bear the cross design used by Pennsylvania Dutch craftsmen.
ABOVE: Replacing the usual curtain rod, a dead branch found on the farm suspends a favorite piece of homespun. The American-made chair came east out of an Iowa girl's childhood.

LEFT: A collection of workaday hats adds a touch of whimsy to a daughter's bedroom, which formerly stood adjacent to the house's summer kitchen; the porthole window was probably originally the space for a flue. RIGHT: Jugs the color of creamware sit atop an English highboy, before one of the old mirrors used throughout the house to stretch available light. The white-painted chair caught Janet's eye in a local eatery because it wasn't "dolled up." She prevailed on the restaurant owner to sell it to her.

ABOVE: A Shaker convention extends seating capacity in a household devoted to collecting likable old chairs.

RIGHT: In the oldest part of the house, a slanted dresser, discovered in one of farm's old barns, provides open storage for Gaudy Welsh china, painted for the first settlers of Bucks County, pottery pitchers, and slipware. Other bright spots in the original kitchen are the 19th-century textile, made in Czechoslovakia for the U.S. trade, and the painted checkerboard floor.

The enduring versatility of American Country is perhaps best demonstrated in homes where eclectic tastes prevail. In new homes built to look old, or old homes stripped to look new, or city homes yearning for a pastoral connection, contemporary applications of the country tradition produce pleasing effects. Collections may be somber or whimsical, massed or presented as individual elements, yet they take on the *Eclectic* appearance of a work of art in discreetly organized spaces. Against modernistically clean settings, the patina of old country furnishings adds not only warmth but also a dose of raw beauty. In another home, sleekly modern furniture is admirably suited to stand among the rustic woodwork and plaster walls of another era. This compatibility of old and new is one more proof of the sophistication of classic design. There is a welcome freshness about the new look. Anything and everything goes with American Country — in caring hands.

Peggy Drexler

A TURN-OF-CENTURY SAN FRANCISCO HOUSE with peaceful views of the garden and the Bay uses country pieces throughout its spare, light-filled interior, magnifying the primitive grandeur of the antiques and endowing the home with an atmosphere of serenity. Viewed against a stark wall, a New England cupboard made in the 1700s invites a modernist's appreciation for its purity of line and time-worn color. Pitchers, jugs, ↘ *San Francisco* plates, and bowls, assembled to herald their hand-fashioned decorations and contours, command attention for their intrinsic merit as well as their utilitarian past. These rustic elements, when brought together in such deceptively simple ways, create a setting that is cosmopolitan yet not so "citified" that it is unwelcoming to visitors.

When Peggy Drexler and her family moved from Manhattan to San Francisco, they reluctantly stored all of the country antiques she had collected over a decade. To her surprise, she found a house in the city that offered her a chance to display her favorite objects in an updated setting.

The shingled dwelling, built in 1904, has a floor plan more reminiscent of the traditions of New England than of California. After years of neglect, the house projected an aura of gloom, with heavy draperies, darkened floors, and papered walls. "But the structure was very special," Peggy recalls. "Rather than redesign it, we decided to strip the house down to its architectural skeleton." Exposing the generous mullioned windows and painting walls and floors a luminous white, Peggy filled the house with light and set up a dramatic backdrop for her cherished furnishings.

"When we were finally able to move the furniture into this house," she says, "I felt I was seeing my old friends again. I was back home."

Peggy departs from familiar country style with her emphasis on brightness, order, and restraint. Instead of spreading collections all over the house, she "exhibits" them in groups as works of primitive art. Her restraint in placing just four yellowware bowls in a cupboard is the key to her wonderful personal style.

Wherever she has moved, from city apartment to country home, contemporary beach house, or her shingled bungalow by the Bay, Peggy has taken her Shaker chairs, scarred farmhouse tables, colorful textiles, and pottery. As with many of us today, her life-style is one of nearly perpetual motion; her devotion to the past through its tangible history gives continuity and serenity.

ABOVE: Plain but handsome, a New England cupboard vies for attention with a Shaker rocker deriving its uncommon grace from a maker mindful that an angel might sit in it.
OPPOSITE PAGE: Baskets, handwoven by Indians, Shakers, and other early Americans, rise above their humble purposes when juxtaposed together in an artistic montage.

LEFT: A sawbuck table from the countryside and two English tables from the sidelines of a cricket pitch provide the practical work surfaces in this office-in-home. RIGHT: Connecticut quilts pieced in the 1800s cushion a deacon's bench; the quilt remnant honors an important farm animal of the past. The English blanket chest with ironstone knobs also dates from the 19th century.

Mullioned bedroom windows, original to the 1904 house, overlook lush gardens originally designed by the eminent California landscape architect Thomas D. Church. Left uncanopied, the reproduction pencil-post bed strikes a contemporary pose, while samplers, a pine bench, and a Shaker blanket rack represent old-fashioned values.

John and Sandy Horvitz

To invest a new house with history, Sandy Horvitz and her husband, John, have linked old and new inside the home and out. A cerulean blue wheelbarrow from Maine and a pale blue wood washtub, both made in the 19th century to serve a farming family, now demonstrate their lasting value on the deck of a country home designed to merge with its natural world. The rustic surfaces, uncomplicated lines, and time-worn traces of paint of Early American ◥ *Long Island* furniture, tools, and equipment are still pleasing to the eye. They are also still practical, serving in a number of surprising ways around the house. Removed from their original settings, primitive forms show off their clean, modern-looking lines, attesting to the enduring design principles they embody. The style is a perfect combination of useful and beautiful.

"A barn without the barn owls"—that was the Horvitzes' objective for their weekend home. Seeking the sense of an old house without the responsibilities that would interfere with their relaxation, they commissioned a newly built house that would look and feel like an old barn, yet meet the needs of a contemporary lifestyle. "I'm a modern person; I don't like cozy little rooms," Sandy says. "I told the architects we wanted a wonderful barn shape, without gimmicks or angles, that you would see on the horizon. I didn't want a building that could be dated. I just wanted a house with classic lines."

Detailing in the house accentuates the barn motif, with pine fascias delineating the white walls, and a simple but soaring fireplace and chimney dominating the living room. The pine floors were sanded and distressed, then stained to acquire the honey-hued veneer of antique wood.

Inside, Sandy filled the rooms with primitive furnishings of Early American houses. I have seen Sandy, a fashion editor who routinely uncovers the best at the couture collections, turn her practiced eye to the acres and acres of antiques on exhibit several times a year in Brimfield, Massachusetts. I am always amazed at how she can speed through this assemblage, pausing only to examine an item of quality. By now she has collected so many painted blue pieces that I call her "the blue lady." Her favorite color is red, but she explains, "The minute I saw all these blue pieces, I wanted to have them." Sandy takes a casual, rather than formal, approach to her home, using her beloved painted pieces to light up each corner. "I once told a friend that he could take the king's castle and his ermine robe," she says. "What I wanted was the peasant's cottage, smock, table, and breadboard."

Soldiers and Sailors, **a 1976 oil-on-wood construction by Betty Parson, has the same primitive appeal as a weathered tin watering can and hand-turned wood bowl and butter ladle from the 1800s.**

RIGHT: The apple ladder from a Maine orchard reaches for the rafters, while a collapsible washstand and a corner cupboard with functional spongeware remind of more down-to-earth tasks. The old toolbox has been converted to a bin for magazines.

OPPOSITE PAGE: A newly built living room has the atmosphere of an old potato barn thanks to pine fascia and floorboards and a collection of old farmhouse necessities in shades of blue. The bucket once collected sap, providing maple syrup for the heart-shaped candy mold.

Flooded with light, an American two-board table handmade with wood nails and bread-board leaves is surrounded by a set of ladder-back chairs from New Hampshire and, for the head of household, an elegant Windsor chair with painted yellow finish. A single-door pie safe, riddled with holes for ventilation, occupies a corner along with a chair featuring a bird-cage back.

ABOVE: A thoroughly modern kitchen shakes the hard edge of new-ness with its array of serviceable stools and tools, table and chairs.
RIGHT: A scrubbed-pine tap table with Hepplewhite legs is set for domestic chores with dough and cheese boards and a wood pitcher once used for storing the leading laundry detergent of the day.

LEFT: **A medley of homespun, wool, and linen checks creates a memorable "red room."**
BELOW: **A country cupboard with its door missing allows a peek into a collection of 19th-century bedding, including a feather-filled blue-and-white homespun tick and a patchwork gingham quilt.**

OPPOSITE PAGE: **An early Pennsylvania cotton rag rug serves its intended purpose in the guest room, while other rugs of the same style act as coverings for built-in sofas.**

The bedroom, over-looking a working farm, bears witness to the 19th-century agri-cultural tradition with an herb-drying rack (now serving as rustic valet), a peach basket, and on the wall, a grain seeder once used to wheel out straight rows of a cash crop. The worn paint finishes of the New York State cupboard and the three-drawer desk add a primitive beauty.

Poolside entertaining gets a welcome jolt from the past with once common household items, including Navajo hand-hammered silver souvenirs from the 1930s, inset with turquoise, called to the table for serving.

Tom Fallon

THE CARPENTER GOTHIC COTTAGE by the sea was built as part of a Methodist health camp in 1875, to make the most of the innocent pleasures of summer. Today, with its gingerbread ornamentation restored and its front porch properly outfitted with wicker, an Amish dry sink, and an old Sears Roebuck swing, the house welcomes the outdoors for Tom Fallon, its present owner. Inside, Fallon, an admitted yard sale connoisseur with a propensity to mix "high

◣ *Long Island*

junk" with pedigree, has enlivened the sober setting with a whimsical collection of Americana. The result is a house with an affectionate respect for its folk past, but with a refreshingly lively sense of humor.

One glance inside Tom Fallon's house promises a weekend of fun for the visitor. An inveterate browser at yard sales, junk shops, and proper

ABOVE: A sing-along upright, découpaged with Victoriana, shows off a Mexican tin cemetery lamp and other yard sale finds.
RIGHT: A deliberate "mishmash of styles" includes a Gothic chair from a Masonic lodge, a wrought-iron garden table from the 1930s, an American brass student lamp, a mid-19th-century lacquered Japanese birdcage, and an English cricket ball.

antiquaries, Tom has furnished every room with his often bizarre finds.

I love meeting someone like Tom who doesn't leave a cookie-cutter stamp on the home. Instead of following the rules, he puts things together in combinations that please him. You can tell he really enjoys doing things like converting beach hats into lampshades for his living room.

"It would not interest me to re-create Victorian rooms per se," says Tom, "but I did want people to know they were in an old house." To make sure he knew the house well enough to reinterpret it without violating its character, he lived in it for several years before starting renovation. Then he installed a new kitchen and bathrooms that continue the sensibility of the carpenter Gothic house with paneled wainscoting and architectural detailing.

The living room, with its rustic stone fireplace and ship captain's handmade paneling, suggested a Victorian lodge, so Tom enhanced the mood, introducing animal skins, old prints, a ship's model, and an old "banger" piano for Saturday night songfests. Upstairs, he inherited a red-painted room and expanded on its aura of drama and mystery.

In his professional life, Tom is the promotion and advertising director for fashion designer Bill Blass; Tom's house is a logical extension of his creative skills. Tom added graining, marbling, and stenciling throughout the house, executing the work himself. A variety of Swedish and English armoires stand among the idiosyncratic Americana Tom has picked up on his travels.

"In fashion there is a thin line between vulgarity and style," Tom asserts. "The same concept is applicable to living spaces as well. I look for objects and furniture that will give life—and individuality."

ABOVE: **Furnished to evoke the atmosphere of a hunting retreat, the living room has animal skins on the floor, oars on the ceiling, and a Victorian sofa with revolutionary pull-out bed feature. A ship's model sits atop the 19th-century Swedish armoire.**

LEFT: The most play-
ful room in the house
has a Venetian spun-
sugar glass chandelier,
a dignified American
sporting portrait, and
salmon-colored walls.
RIGHT: Church pews
provide seating in a
breakfast nook that also
features a Victorian hat
rack, a hand-stenciled
floor, and a tramp art
table lamp made of
Popsicle sticks.

The diversity of Fallon's collection comes together in a single corner display of a metal sculpture of common kitchen chairs, a traditional equestrian portrait found at a yard sale, and a seascape painted by Angus MacPhail, the carpenter who helped renovate the house.

ABOVE AND LEFT:
The two bathrooms are
newly renovated in
keeping with the pe-
riod. One features a
pedestal sink found in a
scrapyard, the other a
gray marble sink res-
cued from a 19th-
century Brooklyn
brownstone. The light
fixtures, copies of ship's
lamps, were designed
to roll with the waves.
OPPOSITE PAGE:
Under a ceiling hand-
stenciled in red to
retain the room's orig-
inal air of mystery, a
Victorian child's bed
and wicker chair have
been given a tortoise-
shell finish.

ABOVE: The guest bedroom comes complete with a pair of spool beds, original to the house and dressed in Victorian crochet work, and a suitcase from the 1920s.

RIGHT: A pair of soaring Gothic French doors in the all-white master bedroom, guarded by an antique metal bulldog, opens onto a sleeping porch.

Mary Emmerling

My house in Bridgehampton, in a section of Long Island where potato fields still dominate the landscape and vast beaches define the shoreline, is home to my favorite country pieces. They are the things I fell in love with over the years as I traveled from place to place trying to learn as much as I could about the phenomenon of American Country.

Wherever I went, my eye would *Bridgehampton, Long Island*

be caught by the wonderful color or design or handiwork in old cupboards, stools and chairs, baskets, gardening whatnot, textiles, folk art figures, souvenirs of the West, and all the rest. It wasn't always easy to get these finds back home—stowing painted benches or a clutch of firkins in a plane's overhead rack can be a challenge. But once that object reached

248

its rightful destination, the effort was soon forgotten. The reward is seeing a genuine emblem of the past in a new and appropriate niche, adding its unique warmth and meaning to the home.

My fondness for ocean beaches goes back to childhood. Every summer, we packed up the family car and headed for Rehoboth Beach, Delaware, for two delightful weeks of life in a seaside community. To this day, I love salt air, sand on wood floors, card games on the porch, almost anything cooked on the outdoor grill, and all the other rites and rituals of the classic American summer.

A few years ago, when I had grown tired of living in a rustic farmhouse with old pipes and unreliable wiring, I decided to find a house that would give me all the modern conveniences but also provide the casual cottage atmosphere and comforts I had grown to love as a girl.

The house I found in Bridgehampton was so close to what I wanted that I thought the builder must have read my mind. As it happened, I discovered later that he had read all of my books. In building new homes, he consciously incorporated "old house" qualities such as pine floors, barn siding on some walls, salvaged ceiling beams, and even authentic country furniture in place of conventional cabinetry for storage.

Not surprisingly, when I moved into this house, my furniture and collections settled into the space without missing a beat. And I loved the sunny location, for it allowed me to plant an herb garden near the kitchen, and along a brick walkway leading to the front door, my American version of that slightly ragtag but romantic English cottage garden.

"No twig chairs!" my children, Samantha and Jonathan, insisted, so I have made

LEFT: **With open-door storage in the house, it's easy to create table settings to match the menu.**
BELOW: **A den lined with barn siding, wired for sound, and full of books and mementoes, serves as the family cocoon on rainy days and winter nights.**
OPPOSITE PAGE: **The painted Ohio corner cupboard, dating from the early 18th century and one of Mary's first finds, holds everyday vessels.**

Pillows and draperies made with 1930s fabric remnants, a ladylike touch in a rustic setting, provide a counterpoint to the bold pattern of a modern overstuffed sofa.

RIGHT: Topiaries and toolbox grace an old farm table set for dinner for eight.
OPPOSITE PAGE: Instead of built-ins, an old English cupboard was called into service, bringing the spirit of Arcadia along with its storage space. A marble top and bottom shelf transformed a simple table into an essential work center.

a few concessions to family reality in dressing up this house in American Country. The beauty of the country approach to home style is that you make your house your own. It is possible to embellish it with meaning and authenticity without sacrificing creature comforts. Your family's circumstances supersede rules.

So, there are plump-cushioned new sofas in both the family den and the main room for entertaining, because we need seats for family members as well as visitors to sink into and relax. And there are no secrets, because all my cupboards and shelves are open, full of the dishes, vases, and other vessels I can admire every day for their primitive beauty, even if I decide not to set the table with them.

My love of the West, as strong as my affection for the sand dunes of the Eastern Seaboard, dates from the visits I made to my uncle's ranch in Wyoming. William Henry Harrison, Sr., who served in the U.S. Congress, had a spread outside of Sheridan, and it was there I learned to ride quarter horses and appreciate the artistry and cultures of American cowboys and Native Americans.

It was this experience that inspired me to give over a corner of my new Yankee homestead to the crafts and traditions of the Old West. The man who built the house neglected to include a corral and a bunkhouse, but imagination can provide what's missing.

In the natural hub of the house, open to the seasons and presided over by a monumental brick fireplace, there are comfortable seats aplenty. An abundance of pillows and flowers completes the welcoming look.

ABOVE RIGHT: At the head of a pine bed of roses, a lace-trimmed tablecloth softens a rustic look.
BELOW RIGHT: The bedside table is a soothing study of nature in a variety of guises.
OPPOSITE PAGE: In a corner of the den, a rodeo banner from the 1940s, sombreros, cowhide throw rugs, and clay water jugs make up an evocative tableau of the Old West.

ABOVE: The screened
porch, a room given
over to the garden in
its furnishings and mo-
tifs, also doubles as a
potting shed.
RIGHT: The pleasing
disarray of a cottage
garden, full of old-
fashioned flowers such
as cosmos and hydran-
gea, greets visitors at
the front door.

Directory

AFTER TEN YEARS OF ASSEMBLING RESOURCES FOR MY BOOKS, I decided it was time to update and revise those from my earlier directories. I was pleased to add new places as well because it shows how the love of American Country has grown and changed.

In this directory you will find sources that frequently reflect the country look through a regional viewpoint or specialty. There is something delightful about the sight of a Texas store that combines Native American crafts with Queen Anne highboys; or a Connecticut shop that specializes in what is now called the Southwest look.

In looking over this new version, I was pleased to see how many country stores and museums devoted to all things American had evolved over the years. Those of us who have admired the simple beauty of a Shaker chair or a Navajo blanket have been content to wait until more and more people discover what we have loved and collected for years.

The most wonderful thing about this directory is that you can select from the various sources and create a classic look that is yours alone. The message I have always tried to communicate to my reader friends is to be willing to take a chance on the unique and unusual. I hope these entries will help you do just that.

ALABAMA

Blackburn-Mastich House
Highway 72, Route 5, Box 84
Athens 35611
(205) 233-4148
American antiques and collectibles.

Country Friends Antiques
3253 Lorna Road
Birmingham 35216
(205) 823-7303
Folk art, quilts, and home furnishings.

Paddlewheel Antiques
3920 Camellia Drive
Mobile 36693
(205) 666-2801
An assortment of late-18th-through 20th-century antiques.

ARIZONA

Al Zuni Indian Trading Co.
7084 Fifth Avenue
Scottsdale 85251
(602) 947-4977
Native American jewelry and crafts.

American Indian Life and
   Legends
121 East Aspen
Flagstaff 86001
(602) 945-2118
(800) 328-6488
Reproductions and original art created by Native American artists. Mediums include prints, porcelain, pewter, and bronze.

Elaine Horwitch Gallery
4211 North Marshall Way
Scottsdale 85251
(602) 945-0791
*American and Southwestern
paintings, graphics, sculpture,
and mixed media.*

Ex Libris Art Books—Design
   Objects
4222 North Marshall Way
Scottsdale 85251
(602) 941-5289
*Books devoted to the arts,
including architecture and design
in the Southwest.*

Main Trail Galleries
7169 Main Street
Scottsdale 85251
(602) 949-9312
*Fine Western Americana,
contemporary and antique
paintings, antique and
contemporary bronzes,
prehistoric pottery, antique
baskets.*

National Native American
   Cooperative
Box 301, San Carlos
Apache Reservation
San Carlos 85550
(602) 475-2229
*A Native American cooperative
representing 2,700 individual
artists from over 100 tribes
throughout the United States and
Canada. A reference guide, The
Native American Directory,
is also available, listing
organizations, events, reserves,
Native American stores, trading
posts, galleries, and more.*

Navajo Silvercrafts
1713 West Buchanan
Phoenix 85007
(602) 253-1594
*Traditional Navajo-style
jewelry.*

Neighbor Lady's Antiques
7014 First Avenue
Scottsdale 85251
(602) 947-6663
*Early American country
furniture, folk art, and quilts.*

Sanders Galleries
6420 North Campbell
Avenue
Tucson 85718
(602) 299-1763
*Traditional Western and
contemporary Southwestern
paintings, jewelry, baskets,
pottery, and rugs.*

Thunderbird Lodge
Box 548
Canyon de Chelly National
Monument
Chinle 86503
(602) 674-5443
*Jeep tours into Canyon de
Chelly. Native American
handmade arts and crafts in the
heart of a Navajo reservation.*

CALIFORNIA
American Country Antiques
3111 North St. Helena
Highway
St. Helena 94574
(707) 963-4308
*Completely restored American
antique furniture, including
tables, chairs, beds, sideboards,
buffets, bookcases, files, dressers,
and highboys.*

The Back Porch
394 East Campbell Avenue
Campbell 95008
(408) 374-4419
*Country antiques, contemporary
folk art, and dried flowers.
Design and construction of hand-
stenciled furniture and wooden
items. Classes on stenciling,
making country hats, and
wreaths.*

Country Pine and Design
1318 Montana Avenue
Santa Monica 90403
(213) 451-0317
Pine furniture, wicker, folk art.

Brenda Cain
1617 Montana Avenue
Santa Monica 90403
(213) 393-3298
*Specializes in one-of-a-kind
vintage items.*

Brush Colorado
1025 Montana Avenue
Santa Monica 90403
(213) 319-0414
Antiques.

Federico
1522 Montana Avenue
Santa Monica 90403
(213) 458-4134
*Native American collectibles,
textiles, jewelry.*

Marjorie Cahan Gallery
P.O. Box 2065
Los Gatos 95031
(408) 356-0023
*Southwestern and Native
American art including
paintings, graphics, textiles,
crafts, and artifacts as well as the
Plains Indian Morning Star quilt
collection of Florence Pullford.*

The Native American Art
   Gallery
215 Windward Avenue
P.O. Box 1020
Venice 90291
(213) 392-8465
*Prehistoric and antique arts of the
American Indian, specializing in
Native arts of the Southwest.*

Nonesuch Gallery
1211 Montana Avenue
Santa Monica 90403
(213) 393-1245
*American Indian artifacts,
cowboy relics, country
primitives, buffalo skulls,
Mexican/Colonial furniture, folk
art, American Indian jewelry,
and textiles.*

Parrish & Sons Antiques
355 Hayes Street
San Francisco 94102
(415) 431-9919
*American antiques, including
American Indian artifacts,
pottery, baskets, beadwork,
weaving, and rugs.*

The Quilt Gallery
1611 Montana Avenue
Santa Monica 90403
(213) 393-1148
Antique quilts, paintings, and folk art.

Richard Mulligan
8471 Melrose Avenue
Los Angeles 90069
(213) 653-0204

Ryan Carey and Mac McLean
2430 Ronda Vista Drive
Los Angeles 90027
(213) 668-0888
Sculpture, sculptural assemblages, as well as one-of-a-kind and limited-edition bronzes by Ryan Carey.

Uncle Tom's American
  Country Antiques
119 South Glassell Street
Orange 92666
(714) 538-3826

Wounded Knee Indian Art
  Gallery
2413 Wilshire Boulevard
Santa Monica 90403
(213) 394-0159
Pueblo pottery, Navajo rugs, Hopi kachina dolls, original paintings, sculpture, graphics, beadwork, fine jewelry, masks, and baskets.

COLORADO
The Antique Shoppe
527 Main Street
Downtown Grand Junction
81501
(303) 242-3532
A complete line of antiques.

Jane Smith
533 East Hopkins Avenue
Aspen 81611
(303) 925-6105
Antique Beacon and Pendleton blankets.

Mark Winter Company
1 Old Durango Road
P.O. Box 1570
Pagosa Springs 81147
(303) 264-5957
Old Navajo rugs and blankets, Saltillo serapes, Pueblo and Rio Grande blankets.

Nizhonie Fabrics, Inc.
East Highway 160,
P.O. Box 729
Cortez 81321
(303) 565-7079
Unique gift items, linen place mats, tea towels, wall hangings, hand-screened material with original Indian designs.

The Ranch
601 East Hopkins Avenue
Aspen 81611
(303) 920-1079
Antique and contemporary furnishings for the home.

Shepler Gallery
103 Bear Creek Avenue
P.O. Box 374
Morristown 80465
(303) 697-5311
Authentic Indian artifacts from the Plains and Southwest Indians: Hopi baskets and kachina dolls; Navajo rugs and sand paintings; Pueblo pottery and paintings.

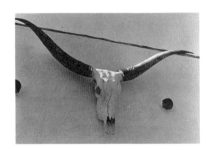

Trash N Treasures
845 Colorado Avenue
Grand Junction 81501
(303) 242-8997
Wicker, furniture of all periods, glassware, original Currier & Ives.

CONNECTICUT
Buckley & Buckley
Box 736, Main Street
Salisbury 06068
(203) 435-9919
William & Mary, country Queen Anne, high country painted furniture and accessories circa 1680–1860. Open daily by chance or by appointment.

Pat Guthman
281 Pequot Avenue
Southport 06490
(203) 259-5743
Primitives, American antiques.

Three Ravens Antiques
Route 44, Main Street
Salisbury 06068
(203) 435-9602
Antiques and decorative accessories; paintings, folk art, country formal furniture, stoneware, decoys, and architectural elements. Open daily by chance or by appointment.

DISTRICT OF
COLUMBIA
Cherishables
1608 20th Street NW
Washington 20009
(202) 785-4087
American antiques, linens, and collectibles.

Counts Western Store
4905 Wisconsin Avenue NW
Washington 20016
(202) 362-1757
Western clothing and boots for men, women, and children.

G. K. S. Bush Inc.
2828 Pennsylvania Ave. NW
Washington 20016
(202) 965-0653
Eighteenth-century American furniture and accessories.

The Indian Craft Shop
Department of the Interior
1801 C Street
Washington 20240
(202) 737-4381
(202) 343-4056
Pottery, jewelry, basketry, sand paintings, and a large collection of Hopi kachinas handmade by Native Americans.

Marston Luce
1314 21st Street NW
Washington 20016
(202) 775-9460
American 18th- and 19th-century furniture, folk art, garden and decorative accessories, quilts and featherbeads.

Rosebud Antiques
1677 Wisconsin Avenue NW
Washington 20007
(202) 965-3355
American antiques and collectibles.

Via Gambaro Studio/Gallery
416 11th Street SE
Washington 20003
(202) 547-8426
Sculpture by Retha Walden Gambaro, contemporary and antique American Indian fine arts and crafts.
By appointment only.

FLORIDA
Cranberry Corner Antiques
203 East Horatio Avenue
Maitland 32751
(407) 644-0363
Fine country and period antiques.

Harrison Antiques
2417 Edgewater Drive
Orlando 32804
(407) 425-6481
Specializing in silver matching, furniture, and Haviland china.

Wenonah Hamasse
777 Donnelly Street
Mt. Dora 32757
(904) 383-1454
Americana and American Indian works from the 18th and 19th centuries.

GEORGIA
The Antique Store of
  Marietta
130 Church Street
Marietta 30060
(404) 428-3376

Deanne Levinson American
  Antiques
2995 Lookout Place NE
Atlanta 30305
(404) 264-0106

The Heritage Collection
The Village at Roswell
  Summit
1085 Holcomb Bridge Road
Roswell 30076
(404) 642-6272
Antiques and primitive folk art.

IDAHO
Blue Haven Antiques
Box 237, 2 miles south
Ketchum 83340
(208) 726-5974
Glass, china, furniture, and primitives.

The Hissing Goose Gallery of
  Fine Americana
Fourth and Leadville
P.O. Box 597
Ketchum 83340
Specializing in 19th- and 20th-century quilts and folk art; also contemporary quilts and fiber arts, Indian baskets, Indian artifacts, and log furniture.

Lorna's Antiques
301 Main Street
Lewiston 83501
(208) 743-5778
Antiques, Western and Indian artifacts.

Marsh's Trading Post
1105 36th Street North
Lewiston 83501
(208) 743-5778
A large collection of Indian material on exhibit and many genuine artifacts for sale.

Natural Woods
P.O. Box 1745
Hailey 83536
(208) 788-9461
Specializing in beds, tables, and chairs.

INDIANA
Jacob Ruby's Granary
R.R. 1, Box 174A
Carthage 46115
(317) 565-6521
Featuring Michael Bonne's restored coppersmith's shop and copper wares.

KENTUCKY
J.W.B. & Co.
226 Holiday Manor Walk
Louisville 40222
(502) 426-6643
Furniture, American folk art.

LOUISIANA
Gallery of the Mesas
2010 Rapides Avenue
Alexandria 71301
(318) 442-6372
Featuring the silk screen, inkless intaglio, and collage works of Charles H. Jeffress.

MAINE
Marie Plummer Goett
Route 9, P.O. Box 1142
Kennebunkport 04046
(207) 967-5282
Fine country antiques, furniture, and accessories of the 17th, 18th, and early 19th century.

Paula Anderson's Blankets
Box 136
North New Portland 04961
(207) 628-2411
Traditional Shaker as well as Indian-inspired large and small woven containers.

Rufus Foshee Antiques
Route 1, P.O. Box 531
Camden 04843
(207) 236-2838

Schuler Antiques
10 High Street
Camden 04843
(207) 236-2770
(617) 738-8309 (winter)
Specializes in 18th- and 19th-century furniture, decorative antique accessories, and rare decoys.

Wabanaki Arts
P.O. Box 453
Old Town 04468
(207) 827-3447
Hand-carved Penobscot war clubs, stone tomahawks, walking sticks, totem poles, beadwork, and quillwork.

MARYLAND
"All of Us Americans"
Bettie Mintz
P.O. Box 5943
Bethesda 20814
(301) 652-4626
Folk art and American antiques.

Archangel Antiques
409 South Talbot Street
St. Michaels 21663
(301) 745-9771
Antique American and English period furniture, china, tableware, rugs, silver, and paintings.

The Country Connection
The Fabian House
8519 Chestnut Avenue
Bowie 20715
(301) 262-6606
(301) 776-9229
Baskets, rugs, beadwork, jewelry, and pottery.

John Newcomer
P.O. Box 130
Funkstown 21734
(301) 790-1327
American antiques.

Village House
103 Cross Street
Chesterton 21620
(301) 778-5766
Antique furniture, folk art, and collectibles.

MASSACHUSETTS
Courtney's
754 Main Street
Osterville 02655
(617) 428-1022
Custom-designed jewelry, baskets, New Mexican pottery, soapstone carvings, Southwest weavings, and sand paintings.

Douglas Antiques
Route 23
South Egremont 01258
(413) 528-5755
Turn-of-the-century American oak furniture: rolltop desks, Hoosiers, dining tables, quilts (1820–1940).

E. G. H. Peter, Inc.
P.O. Box 369
Route 7
Sheffield 01257
(413) 229-8881
American 18th- and 19th-century painted country furniture in original or early surfaces; related decorative accessories.
Open daily by chance or by appointment.

Kuttner Antiques
Route 7
Sheffield 01257
(413) 229-2955
Specializes in 18th- and 19th-century American furniture and decorative accessories.

Lois W. Spring
Ashley Falls Road
Sheffield 01257
(413) 229-2542
Features 18th- and 19th-century American furniture, both country and formal, with appropriate accessories.
Open Saturday and Sunday from ten to five; during the week by chance or by appointment.

Paul Madden
146 Main Street
Sandwich Village 02563
(508) 888-6434
Fine American antiques.

The Splendid Peasant
Route 23/Old Sheffield Road
South Egremont 01258
(413) 528-5755
Specializing in 18th- and 19th-century country furniture, collectibles, decorative smalls, folk art, whimsy, and kitchenalia.

Tranquil Corners Antiques
Whales World Jewelry
49 Sparks Avenue
Nantucket 02584
(508) 228-6000
(508) 228-0848
Country and formal American, Canadian, French, and English antique furniture and accessories. Antique, estate, and new gemstone jewelry. Scrimshaw collection, canes, and quilts.

MINNESOTA

Chippewa Crafts and Gift
  Shop
Red Lake Indian Reservation
Goodridge 56725
(612) 378-4210
(612) 378-4322
*Fancy carved peace pipes,
beadwork, and other items.
Brochure available.*

The Wooden Bird
8600 Kennedy Memorial
  Drive
St. Bonifacius 55375
(612) 446-1613
(800) 328-3615
*Publisher of wildlife and Western
limited-edition lithographs with
retail galleries in Minnesota,
Illinois, and California.*

Woodland Indian Crafts
Minneapolis American Indian
  Center
1530 East Franklin Avenue
Minneapolis 55404
(612) 874-7766
*All Indian handicrafts, beads,
supplies, records, tapes, and
jewelry.*

MISSOURI

Jack Parker Antiques
4652 Shaw at Kings Highway
St. Louis 63110
(314) 773-3320
*Cultural artifacts of the
American Indian (pottery,
baskets, textiles, beadwork) plus
paintings by Midwest and
Southwest artists.*

Spirit of America
1919 Park Avenue
St. Louis 63104
(314) 241-9992
*Specializing in fine American
quilts, 1850–1940. Crystalline
pottery from Arizona, antique
linens, hooked rugs, some
handmade wearable art.
By appointment only.*

MONTANA

Cuts the Rope Gallery
Hays 59527
(406) 673-3304
*Western art by Clarence Cuts the
Rope in oil, pastel, ink, and
watercolor. Wildlife, portraits,
the traditional and contemporary
Indian of the Northern Plains.
By appointment only.*

Doug Allards
Highway 93
St. Ignatius 59865
(406) 745-2951
Antique American Indian art.

Willow Works
425½ South F Street
Livingston 59047
(406) 222-1318
*Traditional willow furniture
handcrafted in materials from
local ranches and along the banks
of the Yellowstone River.
Frames constructed using the
mortise-and-tenon technique.*

NEBRASKA

Anderson/O'Brien Gallery
8724 Pacific Street
Countryside Village
Omaha 68114
(402) 390-0717
*Rare antique prints and original
art from the plains and plateau
area, including 19th-century
American Indian beadwork,
baskets, and related artifacts.*

NEVADA

Sierra Galleries
P.O. Box 5800
Stateline 89449
(702) 588-8500
*Dealers in new and old art of the
American West.*

NEW MEXICO

Cerrilos Saddlery
236 North Guadalupe
Santa Fe 87501
(505) 984-1672
*Handmade saddles and tack;
made-to-order belts, briefcases,
and gift items. Antiques and
reproductions; restorations.*

Chuck Lewis Indian Arts
535 Cordova Road, Suite 111
Santa Fe 87501
(505) 988-9661
*One of the Southwest's largest
collections of Indian posters.
Posters and prints of more than
30 top contemporary Native
American artists.*

Dewey-Kofron Gallery
74 East San Francisco Street
Santa Fe 87501
(505) 982-8478
*Fine, rare Native American and
Hispanic American folk art,
furniture, jewelry, pottery,
textiles, and paintings.*

Doodlets Shop
Don Gaspar Avenue
Santa Fe 87501
(505) 983-3771

Elaine Horwitch Gallery
129 West Palace Avenue
Santa Fe 87501
(505) 988-8997
Contemporary American and Southwestern paintings, graphics, sculpture, and mixed-media art.

El Prado Galleries
El Centro Mall
Water Street at Shelby
Santa Fe 87501
(505) 988-2906
Southwestern, contemporary, and Impressionist paintings and sculpture.

Fenn Galleries Ltd.
1075 Paseo de Peralta
Santa Fe 87501
(505) 982-4631
Specializing in paintings by old Taos and Santa Fe artists; Brandywine, Hudson River, and Ashcan schools; masters of the American West. American bronze and stone sculpture, old pottery, baskets, beadwork, and jewelry of the American Indian.

Gallery of the Old West
201 West San Francisco Street
P.O. Box 5582
Santa Fe 87501
(505) 982-9471
Antique guns, spurs, Indian artifacts, saddles, Western memorabilia, Indian rugs.

Institute of American Indian
Arts Shop
1369 Cerrillos Road
Santa Fe 87501
(505) 988-6281
Nonprofit sales outlet for arts and crafts produced by students and alumni of the National Native American College. Paintings, sculpture, beadwork, quillwork, textiles, weavings, baskets, jewelry; Indian traditional techniques such as costumes.

Jane Smith
110 West San Francisco Street
Santa Fe 87501
(505) 988-4775
Antique Beacon and Pendleton blankets.

La Bodega
667 Canyon Road
Santa Fe 87501
(505) 982-8043
Indian jewelry.

Madrid Earthenware Pottery
Box 300, Main Street
Madrid 87033
(505) 471-3450
Featuring red earthenware pottery by Joni Conrad, decorated blue-and-white animal designs, and work of other fine New Mexican potters.

Millicent Rogers Museum
Store
P.O. Box A
Taos 87571
(505) 758-4316
Native American and Spanish arts and crafts.

Native American Artifacts &
Antiquities, Inc.
125 East Palace Avenue, 10A
Santa Fe 87501
(505) 988-9600
Navajo rugs, Pueblo pottery, kachinas, Indian baskets; paintings, prints, posters, and books on the Southwest.

Oke Oweenge Crafts
Cooperative
P.O. Box 1095
San Juan Pueblo 87566
(505) 852-2372
Traditional Pueblo arts and crafts; specializing in San Juan Pueblo red pottery, embroidery, and weaving.

The Rainbow Man
107 East Palace Avenue
Santa Fe 87501
(505) 982-8706
Finest in American art; Edward S. Curtis photography.

Sower Saddle and Silver
Route 1, Box 225
Belen 87002
(505) 864-3420
Quality leather and silver items in the finest cowboy tradition, including sterling silver buckles, bits, and spurs.

Spider Woman Designs
225 Canyon Road
Santa Fe 87501
(505) 984-0136
Antiques of the 19th and 20th centuries, especially those of the Southwest. Also originally designed clothing with Native American motifs.

NEW YORK

American Hurrah Antiques
766 Madison Avenue
New York 10021
(212) 535-1930
Fine American quilts sold, bought, and appraised.

American Indian Crafts
719 Broad Street
Salamanca 14779
(716) 945-1225
Indian owned and operated. Unique handmade products from New York's Seneca and many other tribes.

Bird in Hand
Barbara Trujillo
Main Street
Bridgehampton 11932
(516) 537-3838

Black Bear Trading Post
P.O. Box 47, Route 9W
Esopus 12429
(914) 384-6786
American Indian arts and crafts: baskets, pottery, beadwork, sterling silver jewelry, moccasins, dolls.

The Common Ground
50 Greenwich Avenue
New York 10011
(212) 989-4178
American Indian jewelry, rugs, pottery, beadwork, basketry, and kachina dolls.

Cut Paper
Eisele Road
Kelly Corners 12445
(914) 586-4261
*Silhouettes and other
paper-cutting arts.
By appointment only.*

English Country Antiques
P.O. Box 1995
Snake Hollow Road
Bridgehampton 11932
(516) 537-0606
*A complete line of English and
American antiques, including
furniture, large and small
cupboards, china, linens, and
American folk art.*

Hirshl & Adler
21 East 70th Street
New York 10021
(212) 535-8810
American antiques.

Jay Johnson Folk Art Gallery
1044 Madison Avenue
New York 10021
*American folk art paintings and
sculpture.*

John Acerno
233 East 77th Street
New York 10021
(212) 737-9331
Antiques and collectibles.

Johnny Jupiter, Inc.
1185 Lexington Avenue
New York 10028
(212) 744-0818
*Antique linens, tableware, and
folk art.*

Judi Boisson American
   Antique Quilts
499 Seventh Avenue
New York 10001
(212) 967-8400
*American antique quilts, folk art,
rugs, and furniture.
By appointment only.*

Judith and James Milne, Inc.
American Country Antiques
506 East 74th Street
New York 10021
(212) 472-0107
American antiques.

Kathy Schoemer
Route 166, at Keeler Lane
North Salem 10560
(914) 669-8464

Kelter & Malce
361 Bleecker Street
New York 10014
(212) 989-6760

Morgan MacWhinnie
520 North Sea Road
Southampton 11968
(516) 283-3366
*American antiques.
By appointment only.*

Otto Fenn
Sag Harbor Antique Shop
P.O. Box 345
Madison Street
Sag Harbor 11963
(516) 725-1732

Robert Kinnaman
Brian Ramaekers
P.O. Box 1140
Wainscott 11975
(516) 537-0779
American antiques.

Sage Street Antiques
Sage Street
Sag Harbor 11963
(516) 725-4402

T. J. Antorino
152 East 70th Street
New York 10021
(212) 628-4330
*American antiques, furnishings,
and accessories.*

Thomas K. Woodard
835 Madison Avenue
New York 10021
(212) 794-9404
*Specializes in American quilts
and antiques.*

V. L. Green Booksellers
19 East 76th Street
New York 10021
(212) 439-9194
*Books on the fine and
decorative arts.*

Wolfman-Gold & Good
   Company
116 Greene Street
New York 10012
(212) 431-1888
*Antique tableware and
furnishings; collectibles antique
and new.*

Zona
97 Greene Street
New York 10012
(212) 925-6750
*New Mexican mission furniture,
ponderosa pine, contemporary
and authentic reproductions,
Navajo rugs.*

NORTH CAROLINA

Griffin's Antiques
5109 Vickery Chadel Road
Greensboro 27407
(919) 454-3362

Philip and Susan Harvey
Route 1, Box 153
Tyner 37980
(919) 221-8426

Willow Oak Antiques
Route 12, Box 3394
Lexington 27292
(919) 764-0192

OHIO

Marjorie Staufer
2244 Remsen Road
Medina 44256
(216) 239-1443

OKLAHOMA

Arrowhead Studio
P.O. Box 1598
Tahlequah 74465
(918) 456-1435
Fine arts, oils, watercolors, and drawings by American Indian and contemporary Western artists. Portraits of notable American Indian subjects.

The Galleria
1630 West Lindsey
Norman 73069
(405) 329-1225
Specializing in Native American and Western art. Painting, sculpture, pottery, weaving, and basketry by leading American artists.

Mister Indian's Cowboy
   Store
1000 South Main
Sapulpa 74066
(405) 224-6511
Everything for the cowboy and the Indian.

Snake Creek Workshop
P.O. Box 147
Rose 74363
(918) 479-8867
Necklaces, earrings, bracelets, hatbands, and other jewelry by Knokovtee Scott, a designer reviving an art form from the temple mound period of the Creek and Cherokee tribes.

OREGON

Lincoln Art Gallery
620 Northeast Highway 101
Lincoln City 97367
(503) 994-5839
Fine arts, prints, art supplies, frames, and unique gifts.

Mission Market Arts and
   Crafts
P.O. Box 638
Pendleton 97821
(503) 276-8772
Indian arts and crafts.

PENNSYLVANIA

Crown and Eagle Antiques,
   Inc.
P.O. Box 181
New Hope 18938
(215) 794-7972
American Indian art; old pawn and fine-quality new jewelry; rugs, basketry, beadwork, weapons, and pottery.

The Dilworthtown Country
   Store
275 Brintons Bridge Road
Westchester 19380
(215) 399-0560
Folk art, antiques.

Jeanne's Turquoise
26 East Main Street
Lititz 17543
(717) 626-1616
Handcrafted American Indian jewelry in sterling silver or 14-carat gold. Beads, Navajo rugs, and baskets.

Jimmy Little Turtle's
217 Fourth Street
New Cumberland 17070
(717) 774-7212
Genuine Indian arts and crafts; antiques of the Old West and East; Large selection of old pawn jewelry from the West.

Pine Springs Antiques
28 Yellow Springs Road
R.D. 3
Malvern 19355
(215) 647-1051
Specializes in primitives.

Theo B. Price, Inc.
Route 191
Cresco 18326
(717) 595-2501
Country store. Folk art.

RHODE ISLAND

Doucrest Indian Trading Post
Summit Road
Exeter 02822
(401) 539-8367
Old and new Native American jewelry and regalia.

Stephen Mack
Chase Hill Farm
Ashaway 02804
(401) 377-2331

SOUTH DAKOTA

Red Hail Gift Shop
Oyate Kin Cultural Society
Highway 18, Box 551
Wagner 57380
Bead and craft work, original paintings and drawings, Sioux-design star quilts and ribbon shirts. Custom orders.

Rings 'n Things
P.O. Box 360
Mission 57555
(605) 856-4851
Native American–made items such as beadwork, porcupine quillwork, and sterling silver jewelry.

TEXAS

Alfies—Ralph F. Willard
3113 Knox Street
Dallas 75205
(214) 559-3962
(214) 826-2584
Specializing in American and Southwest folk art as well as Indian artifacts.

Apple Tree Antiques
Old Ingram Village, Box 742
Ingram 78025
(512) 367-4200
American country pieces. Old branding irons, saddles, sun-bleached steer heads.

Charlie Dunn Boot Co.
2222 College Avenue
Austin 78704
(512) 443-4447
Custom-made boots; domestic and exotic leathers. By appointment only.

The Country Gentleman
1506 Driscoll
Houston 77019
(713) 523-8203
Mennonite and Mexican Colonial furniture and accessories; Tarahumara Indian pottery; American country furniture and accessories. By appointment.

The Garden Shop
1832 Bissonnet
Houston 77005
(713) 524-1172
Specializes in antique garden accessories.

The Gypsy Savage
3012 Phil Sall
Houston 77098
(713) 528-0897
Laces and linens, Victorian and Edwardian dresses and accessories.

Jabberwocky
315 East Main
Fredericksburg 78624
(512) 997-7071
Old and new textiles, vintage clothing, replicas of vintage designs.

Plain & Simple
119 West San Antonio Street
Fredericksburg 78624
(512) 997-7488
Country antiques, Texas primitives, and appropriate accessories.

Provitt & Brown
5350 West Lover's Lane
Dallas 75209
(214) 351-6555
Folk art.

Room Service
4354 Lover's Lane
Dallas 75225
(214) 369-7666
Antiques, folk art.

The Settlers Antiques
725 North Main
Boerne 78006
(512) 249-8919
Hill country antiques mixed with New England shipments.

VERMONT

The Store
Route 100, Box 118
Waitsfield 05673
(802) 496-4465

VIRGINIA

Devonshire
6 North Madison Street
Middleburg 22117
(703) 687-5990
Specializes in garden accessories and birdhouses.

WASHINGTON

Akers Taxidermist
1303 Astor Street
Bellingham 98225
(206) 734-1085
Indian-type drums, leather paintings, black bear and other fur rugs.

Sacred Circle Gallery of
   American Indian Art
2223 Fourth Avenue
Seattle 98121
(206) 223-0072
Featuring fine traditional and contemporary American Indian artists.

Seattle Indian Arts and Crafts
617 Second Avenue
Seattle 98104
(206) 623-2252
Crafts made by Native Americans.

Suquamish Museum Store
P.O. Box 498
Sandy Hook Road
Suquamish 98392
(206) 598-3311
Specializing in traditional Coast Salish arts and crafts, both replicas and works by living artists and craftspeople.

WYOMING

Big Horn Taxidermy
5060 Coffeen
Sheridan 82801
(307) 672-2813
Custom taxidermy work.

The Boardwalk, Inc.
Route 1, Box 433
Laramie 82070
(307) 742-3977
A large selection of Indian crafts; custom-made harness and saddlery.

Fort Washakie Trading Co.
R.V. Greeves Art Gallery
Wind River Indian
Reservation
P.O. Box 428
Fort Washakie 82514
(307) 332-3557
American Indian arts and crafts; antique Indian collector's pieces.

Jackson Hole Furniture
1090 South Highway 89
Jackson 83001
(307) 733-7503
Custom shop specializing in rawhide chairs made from cowhide.

Lodgepole Furniture Mfg.
S.R. Box 15
Jackson 83001
(307) 733-3199
Pole and rawhide furniture made with lodgepole pine.

Wyoming Bronze, Inc.
2425 Mountain View Road
Cody 82450
(307) 587-6591
Western and wildlife bronzes, prints, and prints by well-known artists.

◣ *Museums*

ALABAMA

Birmingham Museum of Art
2000 8th Avenue North
Birmingham 35203
(205) 254-2565
Art of the Old West. Bronze sculptures, paintings, and lithographs. Native American art and artifacts from the Northwest Coast, Plains, Southwest, and Alabama Mound Culture tribes, including clothing, accessories, baskets, pottery, headdresses, masks, and blankets.

The Fine Arts Museum of the
    South
Museum Drive
Mobile 36608
(205) 342-4642
Collections of 19th- and 20th-century American paintings and prints, sculpture, Southern decorative arts from the 19th century.

ARIZONA

Casa Grande Ruins National
    Monument and Visitors
    Center
P.O. Box 518
Coolidge 85228
(602) 723-3172
Some 60 prehistoric sites, preserving a small sample of the remains of the once-widespread Hohokam civilization, the prehistoric Native American farmers of the Gila Valley.

Colorado River Indian Tribes
    Museum
Route 1, Box 23B
Parker 85344
(602) 669-9211
A collection dealing with the prehistory and history of the four tribes of the reservation: Mojave, Chemehuevi, Navajo, and Hopi.

Desert Caballeros Western
    Museum
P.O. Box 1446
20 North Frontier Street
Wickenburg 85358
(602) 684-2272
The museum's large collection includes a Hall of History, period rooms, street scenes, a Mineral Room, and a Native American Room dealing with the Wickenburg area, as well as a Western Art Gallery containing bronzes and paintings by past and present Western masters.

Grand Canyon National Park
    Study Collection
P.O. Box 129
Grand Canyon 86023
(602) 638-7769
Collection of material on the Grand Canyon, including prehistoric and historic artifacts, natural history specimens, documents, photographs, and art.

Mohave Museum of History
    and Arts
400 West Beale Street
Kingman 86401
(602) 753-3195
A collection of Native American basketry, pottery, and beadwork from the Hualapai and Mojave tribes.

Museum of Northern
    Arizona
Route 4, Box 720
Flagstaff 86001
(602) 774-5211
Collections dealing with archaeology, ethnology, geology, paleontology, zoology, botany, and Native American and Southwestern arts and crafts. A gift shop carries contemporary Southwestern Native American arts and crafts; a bookshop specializes in books and posters of the Southwest.

Navajo National Monument
    Visitor Center
Tonalea 86044
(602) 672-2366
Guided hikes during the summer months to Native American cliff dwellings ruins, and a museum with exhibits on the prehistoric Anasazi people and a smaller exhibit dealing with contemporary Navajos of the area.

Pioneer Arizona
Interstate 17 at Pioneer Road
Phoenix 85061
(602) 993-0210
Reconstruction of a typical Arizona town of the late 19th century, with 26 buildings.

Pueblo Grande Museum
4619 East Washington Street
Phoenix 85034
(602) 275-3452
A prehistoric Hohokam ruin, a permanent exhibit area explaining the Hohokam, and a changing gallery featuring various Southwestern Native American groups.

ARKANSAS

Arkansas Territorial
    Restoration
Third and Scott Streets
Little Rock 72201
(501) 371-2348
Four mid-19th-century restored houses with period furnishings; also an 1850s log house

CALIFORNIA

Cabots Old Indian Pueblo
    Museum
67616 East Desert View
    Avenue
Desert Hot Springs 92240
(619) 329-7610
Using only his hands, the earth, and cast-off materials, Cabot Yerxa erected this 35-room Hopi structure over a period of 20 years.

California State Indian
    Museum
2618 K Street
Sacramento 95816
(916) 324-0539
One of the largest collections of California Native American baskets in the state.

Clarke Memorial Museum
240 E Street
Eureka 95501
(707) 443-1947
A collection of over 1,500 baskets from the Yurok, Karok, and Hupa tribes of northwestern California; dance regalia and stonework from that area.

Julian Pioneer Museum
2811 Washington Street
Julian 92036
(619) 765-0227
Local Native American baskets, ollas, and artifacts.

Lake County Historical
    Museum
225 North Forbes Street
Lakeport 95453
(707) 263-4555
Collections and exhibits on the Pomo Indian tribe, including an outstanding basket collection.

Maturango Museum of
    Indian Wells Valley
Box 1776
Ridgecrest 93555
(619) 446-6900
Local Native American artifacts and displays along with some mining artifacts.

Natural History Museum of
    Los Angeles County
900 Exposition Boulevard
Los Angeles 90007
(213) 744-3430
Collection of ethnological and archaeological artifacts of Western Native Americans.

Pio Pico Museum
6003 Pioneer Boulevard
Whittier 90606
(213) 695-1217
A 13-room 1852 adobe building containing furnishings from the 1850s–1870s.

San Diego Museum of Man
1350 El Prado
San Diego 92101
Southwestern Native American archaeology and ethnology, physical anthropology, photographs, and library.

Southwest Museum
234 Museum Drive
Los Angeles 90065
(213) 221-2163
Prehistoric, historic, and contemporary Native American art and artifacts; facilities include a research library and a museum store. Located at 4605 North Figuerora, three blocks from the museum proper, is the Casa de Adobe, a re-creation of an 1850s-era Spanish California hacienda with period furnishings and an exhibition gallery.

Will Rogers State Historic
    Park
14253 Sunset Boulevard
Pacific Palisades 90272
Will Rogers's ranch home. Paintings and sculptures by Charles M. Russell, examples of Native American work, primarily Navajo rugs. Open for tours daily.

COLORADO

Baca & Bloom Houses
Pioneer Museum
On the Santa Fe Trail
300 East Main Street
P.O. Box 472
Trinidad 81082
(303) 846-7217
A Colorado Historical Society regional museum complex featuring two restored houses. The adobe, two-story, nine-room, territorial-style Baca house displays Spanish Colonial objects; outlying adobe buildings house a Pioneer Museum and exhibits of Western expansion. The Bloom House, an 1880s Second Empire mansion, displays Victorian objects in a Southwestern setting.

Colorado Historical Society
The Colorado Heritage
    Center
1300 Broadway
Denver 80203
(303) 866-3682
Artifacts from Native American Plains tribes, especially from the people of the Southern and Central plains. Fine arts collection includes most of the works and materials from the studios of Western artists Charles Stobie and Robert Lindneux, among others.

Denver Art Museum
100 West 14th Avenue
Parkway
Denver 80204
(303) 575-2256
(303) 575-2793
Approximately 15,000 Native American objects, covering most tribal groups of the United States and Canada.

Denver Museum of Natural
    History
City Park
Denver 80205
(303) 370-6357
*Contains a Native American
collection.*

Koshare Indian Museum
115 West 18th Street
La Junta 81050
(303) 384-4801
*Native American baskets,
beadwork, and arts and crafts, as
well as over 400 paintings by
Native American and Western
artists.*

ProRodeo Hall of Champions
    and Museum of the
    American Cowboy
101 ProRodeo Drive
Colorado Springs 80919
*The hall features two multimedia
theaters presenting the history of
cowboys and the rodeo; the
museum collection consists of
cowboy artifacts and rodeo
champions' artifacts.*

CONNECTICUT
Buttolph-Williams House
249 Broad Street
Wethersfield 06109
(203) 529-0460
*Built in 1692, a historic house
containing period furnishings and
kitchen equipment.*

Farmington Museum
37 High Street
Farmington 06032
(203) 677-9222
*Historic Stanley-Whitman
house, built in 1660, with period
furnishings, exhibits of local
history, flower and herb gardens.*

The Guilford Keeping Society
Boston Street
Guilford 06437
(203) 453-3176
*Exhibits of local history,
documents, and costumes on
display in a house built in 1736.*

Hempstead House
Hempstead Street
New London 06320
(203) 443-7949
*A 17th-century historic home
with furnishings and decorations
of the period.*

Henry Whitfield State
Historical Museum
Old Whitfield Street
Guilford 06437
(203) 453-2457
*The oldest dwelling in New
England, this house built in 1639
contains 17th- and 18th-century
furnishings.*

Hyland House
84 Boston Street
Guilford 06437
(203) 453-9477
*A historic house built in 1660,
with period furnishings.*

Mystic Seaport
Route 27
Greenmanville Road
Mystic 06355
(203) 536-2631
*A 17-acre maritime museum that
re-creates the 19th-century
seacoast community. With four
major historic vessels, formal
museums, and working
craftspeople.*

Nathan Hale Homestead
South Street
South Coventry 06238
(203) 742-6917
*A ten-room Georgian-style home
built in 1776 and decorated with
period furnishings.*

Putnam Cottage
243 East Putnam Avenue
Greenwich 06830
(203) 869-9697
*Built in 1690, this house was
used by General Israel Putnam
during the Revolutionary war.*

Stratford Historical Society
    Museum
967 Academy Hill
Stratford 06497
(203) 378-0630
*The historic Judson house, built
in 1723, contains period
furnishings and exhibits relating
to local history.*

Tantaquidgeon Indian
    Museum
1819 Norwich–New London
    Turnpike
Uncasville 06382
(203) 848-9145
*Preserves and perpetuates the
history and traditions of the
Mohegan and other Native
American tribes. Displays
include quillwork, bead-
work, pottery, baskets,
and rugs.*

Webb-Deane-Stevens
    Museum
211 Main Street
Wethersfield 06109
(203) 529-7371
*Three authentically restored and
decorated 18th-century houses
with early furniture.*

Wethersfield Historical
    Society
150 Main Street
Wethersfield 06109
(203) 529-7656
*An early 19th-century house
containing exhibits of local
history, household and farm
equipment. The society also
maintains the John Hurlbutt
House, the James Francis House,
and the Old Warehouse.*

The Windsor Historical
    Society and Wilson
    Museum
96 Pallisade Avenue
Windsor 06095
(203) 688-3813
*The historic Fyler House, built
in 1640; period furnishings and
local historic displays.*

DELAWARE
The Corbit Sharp House
Main Street
Odessa 19730
(302) 378-2681
*The historic house, built in
1772, contains period rooms and
decorative arts of the 18th and
19th centuries.*

The Hagley Museum
Greenville
Wilmington 19807
(302) 658-2401
*A 19th-century industrial
community located on 200 acres
of wooded land, with museum
building, mill network of
buildings, and gardens.*

Henry Francis du Pont
Winterthur Museum and
    Gardens
Winterthur 19735
(302) 656-8591
*Collections of American
decorative arts from 1640 to
1840, displayed in more than
175 rooms, exhibit areas, and 60
acres of planted gardens;
examples of architecture,
furniture, textiles, and
needlepoint.*

DISTRICT OF COLUMBIA
National Gallery of Art
Constitution Avenue/6th
    Street NW
Washington 20565
(202) 737-4215
*Edgar William and Bernice
Chrysler Garbisch Collection of
folk art; also additional
collections of 18th- and 19th-
century American oil paintings,
drawings, and watercolors.*

Smithsonian Institution
Washington 20560
(202) 381-5855
*Collections and exhibitions,
housed in several buildings,
include the Freer Gallery of Art
—19th- and early 20th-century
American works; the National
Museum of History and
Technology—folk art, clocks,
tools, textiles, and ceramics; the
National Collection of Fine Arts
—American paintings, sculpture,
and graphic art from the 18th
century to the present; and
the Renwick Gallery—
contemporary and historic
American crafts, decorative arts,
and design.*

FLORIDA
San Augustin Antiquo
P.O. Box 1987
St. Augustine 32084
(904) 824-6383
*Restored 18th-century Spanish
colonial village; craft
demonstrations.*

GEORGIA
High Museum of Art
1280 Peachtree Street NW
Atlanta 30309
(404) 892-3600
*Collections of 18th- to 20th-
century American paintings,
decorative arts, and furniture.*

INDIANA
Museum of Indian Heritage
6040 De Long Road
Indianapolis 46254
(317) 293-4488
*A collection primarily of material
from the Northwest Woodland,
Southwest, and Plains culture
areas; rich in beadwork, pottery,
and basketry.*

President Benjamin Harrison
    Home
1230 North Delaware Street
Indianapolis 46202
(317) 631-1898

William Hammond Mathers
    Museum
Indiana University
601 East Eighth Street
Bloomington 47405
*A museum of anthropology,
history, and folklore; collections
include examples of Southwest
Native American basketry, pots
and potsherds, rugs, and
ceremonial artifacts.*

IOWA

Effigy Mounds National
   Monument
Box K
McGregor 52157
(319) 873-2356
*The monument preserves a
prehistoric Native American
mound; a museum contains
artifacts excavated from the
mounds.*

Norwegian-American
   Museum
502 West Water Street
Decorah 52101
(319) 382-9681
*A museum complex illustrating
the history of early Norwegian
immigrants. Includes a museum
building, an outdoor area with
pioneer homes and schoolhouse,
and industrial exhibits of early
agriculture, carpentry, and
blacksmithing.*

KANSAS

Last Indian Raid in Kansas
   Museum
258 South Penn
Oberlin 67749
(913) 475-2712
*A museum based on western
Kansas pioneers. General
frontier artifacts with excellent
Native American displays.*

Old Cowtown Museum
1871 Sim Park Drive
Wichita 67203
(316) 264-0671
*A re-created early frontier village
featuring 36 buildings that
represents Wichita during its
early settlement and growth
period.*

KENTUCKY

Duncan Tavern
Historic Center
Public Square/Highway 68
Paris 40361
(606) 987-1788
*Two historic buildings, a tavern
and dwelling, both with period
furnishings.*

Shaker Village at Pleasant Hill
Route 4
Harrodsburg 40330
(606) 734-5411
*A restored 19th-century Shaker
village with 27 original buildings
on 3,000 acres of farmland;
includes furnished dwellings,
shops, meetinghouse, post office,
craft demonstrations.*

MAINE

Parson Smith Homestead
River Road
South Windham 04082
(207) 892-5315
*A historic eight-room house built
in 1764, with period furnishings.*

Wilson Museum
P.O. Box 196
Castine 04421
(207) 326-8753
*Native American artifacts from
California, Plains Native
American beadwork, Pueblo
pottery, fine Western saddles
collected before 1900.*

MARYLAND

Hammond-Harwood House
19 Maryland Avenue
Annapolis 21401
(301) 269-1714
*Historic house built in 1774 by
colonial architect William
Buckland, with period
furnishings.*

Southerly Mansion
Hollywood 20636
(301) 373-2280
*Eighteenth-century manor house,
with working plantation.
By appointment only.*

MASSACHUSETTS

Adams National Historic Site
135 Adams Street
Quincy 02169
(617) 773-1177
*The Adams family residence,
with family heirlooms and
furniture, garden, and carriage
house.*

Colonel John Ashley House
Cooper Hill Road
Ashley Falls 01222
(413) 229-8600
*Built in 1765, the house has
period furnishings and an herb
garden.*

Concord Museum
Route 2A/Lexington Road
   and Cambridge Turnpike
Concord 01742
(617) 369-9609
*The museum contains period
rooms and dioramas of famous
battles. Emerson's and Thoreau's
studies are reproduced here.*

The Fairbanks House
East Street and Eastern
   Avenue
Dedham 02026
(617) 326-1170
*The oldest wood frame house in
the United States, inhabited from
1636 to 1903, with period family
furnishings.*

Hancock Shaker Village
U.S. 20, Box 898
Hancock 01237
Pittsfield 01201
(413) 443-0188
*A restored settlement of 21
buildings with collections of
Shaker-made furnishings,
artifacts, and farm implements.
Among the farm buildings is the
1826 Round Stone Barn.*

Museum of Fine Arts
497 Huntington Avenue
Boston 02115
(617) 267-9300
*M. and M. Karolik Collections
of American folk art and
primitive paintings.*

Nantucket Historical
   Association
Old Town Hall
Union Street
Nantucket 02557
(505) 228-1894
*The association provides
information on other historic
buildings and homes.*

Orchard House
Route 2A/399 Lexington Road
Concord 01742
(617) 369-4118
Home of the Alcott family during the 19th century; combines two houses built in 1650 and 1730.

Paul Revere House
19 North Square
Boston 02116
(617) 523-1676
Historic house of one of America's early patriots. Dates from 1680 and contains period furnishings.

Peabody Museum of Archaeology and Ethnology
Harvard University
11 Divinity
Cambridge 02138
The oldest museum in the nation devoted exclusively to anthropology; some of the oldest and most complete Native American collections in the world. All major cultural areas are represented; strongest are the Southwest, Northwest Coast, and Plains areas.

Salem Witch House
310½ Essex Street
Salem 01970
(617) 744-5217
The home of Magistrate Jonathan Corwin during the Salem witch trials. Contains 17th-century furnishings.

Society for the Preservation of New England Antiquities
141 Cambridge Street
Boston 02114
(617) 227-3956
Located in the Harrison Gray Otis house, dating from 1795, collections of regional decorative arts, architectural prints, photographs, toys, and needlework. The society also maintains historic houses in Massachusetts, Maine, New Hampshire, Connecticut, and Rhode Island.

MICHIGAN
Detroit Museum of the Arts
5200 Woodward Avenue
Detroit 48202
(313) 833-7900
The Robert Tanahill Wing has American decorative arts, paintings, and sculpture from the late 17th century through the early 20th.

Greenfield Village and Henry Ford Museum
Dearborn 48121
(313) 271-1620
A village situated on 260 acres, with over 100 restored buildings, from all over the United States, tracing three centuries of American arts and skills; examples of Americana in the decorative, mechanical, and industrial arts.

MINNESOTA
Mille Lacs Indian Museum
Star Route Box 192
Onamia 56359
Artifacts and art from the Ojibway tribe.

The Minnesota Historical Society
690 Cedar Street
St. Paul 55101
(612) 296-6126
A large collection of Native American artifacts. Predominantly Sioux and Ojibway, some Southwestern and Pacific Northwest.

Pipestone National Monument
Box 727
Pipestone 56164
(507) 825-5463
Upper Plains Native American artifacts, primarily pipes and effigies carved from pipestone.

MISSOURI
Museum of Anthropology
100 Swallow Hall
University of Missouri
Columbia 65211
(314) 882-3764
Small collections of contemporary Southwestern Native American jewelry and ceramics.

MONTANA
Yellowstone County Museum
Logan Field
Billings 59101
(406) 248-6341
Native American artifacts, collections of antique moccasins, Western paintings, dioramas, old guns, and horse-drawn vehicles. Also a class L-7 steam train.

NEBRASKA
Museum of the Fur Trade
HC 74, Box 18
Chadron 69337
(308) 432-3843
Firearms, silver, textiles, cutlery, beads, and other trade artifacts, plus fine North American Native American items, trappers' equipment, and early Southwestern horse gear, weapons, and traveling outfits, all related to the North American fur trade.

Willa Cather Historical Center
338 North Webster Street
Red Cloud 68970
(402) 746-3285
A branch museum of the Nebraska State Historical Society. Willa Cather's childhood home, restored and refurnished, and five other properties associated with the regional writer's life and works. The center also maintains an archive of Cather books, manuscripts, documents, and photographs.

NEW HAMPSHIRE
The Currier Gallery of Art
192 Orange Street
Manchester 03104
(603) 669-6144
Exhibits of American decorative arts, including pewter, glass, and paintings.

New Hampshire Historical
Society
30 Park Street
Concord 03301
(603) 225-3381
*Four period rooms with
collections of New Hampshire
decorative arts and changing
exhibits.*

Shaker Village, Inc.
Canterbury 03224
(603) 783-9822
*A village with a museum located
in an old meetinghouse built in
1742. Guided tours of other
buildings on the site.*

NEW JERSEY
The Gund Collection of
Western Art
14 Nassau Street
P.O. Box 449
Princeton 08542
(609) 921-3626
*A traveling exhibition of
American Western art, including
over 60 paintings, watercolors,
etchings, lithographs, and bronze
sculptures by Frederic
Remington, Charles Russell,
Alfred Jacob Miller, Albert
Bierstadt, and others of the Old
West era.*

Historic Town of Smithville
Smithville 08201
(609) 652-7777
*A re-created mid-19th-century
southern New Jersey town, with
exhibits in 40 buildings; period
furnishings and craft
demonstrations.*

Monmouth County
Historical Association
70 Court Street
Freehold 07728
(201) 462-1466
*The museum building has
collections of furniture, paintings,
toys, and weapons. Also
maintained are four historic
18th- and 19th-century
furnished houses.*

Morristown National
Historic Park
Morristown 07960
(201) 221-0311
*The 18th-century Ford mansion,
Wick Farm of 1750, and five
reconstructed huts.*

Old Dutch Parsonage and the
Wallace House
38 Washington Place
Somerville 08876
(201) 725-1015
*Two 18th-century houses with
typical 18th- and 19th-century
furnishings.*

NEW MEXICO
Albuquerque Museum
2000 Mountain Road NW
P.O. Box 1293
Albuquerque 87103
(505) 766-7878
*Spanish Colonial artifacts from
the 15th to the 19th century,
territorial artifacts, Western art
with emphasis on New Mexico
and the Southwest. Hispanic arts
and crafts, limited collection of
New Mexico Native American
materials, photo archive with
45,000 images of Albuquerque
from 1868 to the present.*

Aztec Historical Museum
125 North Main
Aztec 87410
(505) 334-9551
*Comprehensive exhibits of
ancient Native American artifacts
and Navajo arts and crafts. Four
rooms of period furnishings,
numerous indoor and outdoor
exhibits of historic interest.*

Aztec Ruins National
Monument
P.O. Box U
Aztec 87410
(505) 334-6174
*A museum and self-guiding trail
that explains the life of the
ancient Anasazi people who
lived here.*

Bent Gallery Museum
18 Bent Street
Taos 87571
(505) 758-2376
*Western art featuring works of
Taos founders and other early
Taos artists. Native American
artifacts, basketry, and pottery.*

Blackwater Draw Museum
2029 Enmu
Portales 88130
(505) 562-2306
*A collection of Native American
artifacts.*

Coronado State Monument
P.O. Box 95
Bernalillo 87004
(505) 867-5351
A walking tour through the ruins of a 14th-century pueblo, a visitors' center housing original Pueblo painted murals, and a main exhibit room describing the life-styles of Pueblo Native Americans and Spanish Colonials and their interactions.

Deming Luna Mimbres
   Museum
301 South Silver
Deming 88030
(505) 546-2382
Native American artifacts, including Mimbres pottery, baskets, chuck wagon equipment, saddles, and tack. Also a Quilt Room and Doll Room.

Farmington Museum
302 North Orchard
Farmington 87401
(505) 327-7701
Material relevant to the social and cultural history of Farmington and the Four Corners area. Includes Navajo, Hispanic, and Anglo cultures.

Greater Grants Chamber of
   Commerce Museum
500 West Santa Fe Avenue
Grants 87020
(505) 287-4802
A small museum with art, artifacts, pottery, mineral, and basket collections from the area.

Indian Pueblo Cultural
   Center
2401 12th Street NW
Albuquerque 87102
(505) 843-7270
(505) 843-7271
The Pueblo Indian Museum tells the story of the Pueblo people from prehistoric times to the present from the Native American point of view. Facilities also include a Native American restaurant and a gift shop featuring handmade items.

Log Cabin Museum
Main Street, Box 83
Pinos Altos 88053
(505) 388-1882
Native American artifacts from the area as well as articles connected with gold mining.

Los Alamos Historical
   Society and Museum
1921 Juniper
P.O. Box 43
Los Alamos 87544
(505) 662-4493
A museum devoted to the history and culture of the Pajarito Plateau.

Maxwell Museum of
   Anthropology
University of New Mexico
Albuquerque 87131
(505) 277-4404
Archaeological and ethnographic collections of Native North America with emphasis on the Southwest. Dorothy and Gilbert Maxwell collection of Southwestern weaving, mid-20th-century Hopi kachinas, basketry (especially Northwest Coast), and Frances Newcomb sand painting drawings.

Millicent Rogers Museum
P.O. Box A
Taos 87571
(505) 758-2462
Anthropology and art museum of prehistoric and historic Southwestern and Plains Native American art and material culture, religious and secular arts of Hispanic New Mexico. Family collection of Maria Martinez, potter of San Ildefonso.

Museum of New Mexico
Museum of International
   Folk Art
Box 2087
Santa Fe 87501
(505) 827-6450
A museum of history, anthropology, fine arts, and folk art, with Native American, Hispanic, and Anglo-American art and artifacts of Southwestern origin. Includes collection of Alexander Girard.

Old Cienega Village Museum
Route 2, Box 214
Santa Fe 87501
Situated on 350 acres with numerous buildings, among them a placita house with Spanish Colonial furnishings, an 18th-century house and functional buildings, a Sierra mountain village depicting life in the 18th and 19th centuries, and a reconstructed morada penitente meetinghouse.

The Old Coal Mine Museum
The Turquoise Trail
Highway 14, Madrid Star
  Route
Madrid 87010
(505) 473-0743
Three acres of original buildings and displays of artifacts and equipment related to the historic railroading and mining activities of the region.

Old Mill Museum
P.O. Box 58
Cimarron 87714
(505) 376-2913
History and artifacts of early Cimarron, the Santa Fe Trail, and the area's first settlers and ranchers. Also Ute and Jicarilla Apache artifacts.

Pueblo of Acoma
P.O. Box 309
Pueblo of Acoma 87034
Acoma, or "Sky City," is the oldest continuously inhabited city in the United States.

Roswell Museum and Arts
  Center
100 West 11th Street
Roswell 88201
(505) 622-4700
Municipal museum specializing in art and artists of New Mexico. Southwestern painting, sculpture, and graphics as well as extensive Native American exhibits.

San Miguel Church
401 Old Santa Fe Trail
Santa Fe 87501
(505) 983-3974
The original church was built about 1610 and is the oldest church still in active use in the United States. Inside are original skin paintings, statues, and other artworks dating from the 18th and 19th centuries.

Silver City Museum
312 West Broadway
Silver City 88061
(505) 538-5921
An extensive collection of pottery and metalwork of the Casas Grandes Indians of southern Arizona and northern Mexico.

Tularosa Village Historical
  Museum
501 Fresno
Tularosa 88352
(505) 585-2057
Collections representing three cultures—Native American, Spanish/Mexican, and Anglo—concentrating on the Tularosa Village area.

The University Museum
New Mexico State University
Box 3564
Las Cruces 88003
(505) 646-3739
The museum's emphasis is on Southwestern archaeology, ethnology, and history, especially southern New Mexico and northern Mexico.

Wheelwright Museum of the
  American Indian
704 Camino Lejo
Santa Fe 87502
(505) 982-4636
Four exhibits a year feature traditional and contemporary Native American arts, crafts, and culture. Case Trading Post and the museum shop offer a wide variety of Native American arts and crafts.

NEW YORK

American Museum of
  Natural History
Central Park West
  at 79th Street
New York 10024
(212) 873-1300
The Anthropology Department has extensive archaeological and ethnographic collections of North American Indian artifacts.

Brooklyn Museum
188 Eastern Parkway
Brooklyn 11238
(718) 638-5000
Four centuries of American decorative arts displayed in 30 period rooms, with collections of American paintings, sculpture, and Native American artifacts.

Cooper-Hewitt Museum
2 East 91st Street
New York 10028
(212) 860-6898
Collections of decorative arts, including textiles, furniture, ceramics, glass, woodwork, drawings, prints, architectural ornaments, and American wallpapers from the 18th century.

Fenimore House
Lake Road
Cooperstown 13326
(607) 547-2533
Collections of American folk art, Hudson River School paintings, and James Fenimore Cooper memorabilia.

Huguenot Historical Society,
  Inc.
Huguenot Street
New Paltz 12561
(914) 255-1660
Seventeenth-century stone house and French church, with period furnishings.

Metropolitan Museum of Art
Fifth Avenue at 82nd Street
New York 10021
(212) 879-5500
Collections of 18th- and 19th-century American paintings and sculpture, and an entire wing dedicated to American decorative arts dating from the 16th century.

Museum of American Folk Art
61 West 62nd Street
New York 10023
(212) 977-7170
Exhibitions of American folk art from the late 17th century through the 20th, with collections of naive paintings, carvings, tools, signs and symbols, textiles, and pottery reflecting the inventiveness of the self-taught artist.

Museum of the American
Indian
Broadway at 155th Street
New York 10032
(212) 283-2420
*Devoted to the collection,
preservation, study, and
exhibition of all things connected
with the anthropology of the
aboriginal peoples of North,
Central, and South America.*

Ontario County Historical
Society
55 North Main Street
Canandaigua 14424
(716) 394-4975
*Mary Clark Thompson
collection of Southwest and
Pacific Coast Native American
baskets.*

Shaker Museum
Shaker Museum Road
Old Chatham 12136
(518) 794-9105
*The country's oldest and largest
collection of Shaker artifacts.*

Sleepy Hollow Restorations
Sunnyside, Phillipsburg
Manor, and Van Cortland
Manor headquarters
150 White Plains Road
Tarrytown 10591
(914) 631-8200
*Restorations representing the
history of the Hudson River
valley over the last three
centuries; each reflects its period
and the differing life patterns
along the Hudson.*

Thomas Paine Cottage
North and Paine Avenues
New Rochelle 10802
(914) 632-5376
*The writer-patriot's 18th-century
farmhouse.*

NORTH CAROLINA

Historic Edenton
Edenton 27932
(919) 482-3663
*Five restored 18th- and 19th-
century buildings: three houses
with period furnishings, a
courthouse and church still
in use.*

Museum of Early Southern
Decorative Arts
924 South Main Street
Winston-Salem 27101
*Fifteen period rooms, with
furniture and objects of the South
from the 18th to the early 19th
century.*

Old Salem
Old Salem, Drawer F
Winston-Salem 27108
(919) 723-3688
*Restored 18th- and 19th-century
Moravian town with eight
exhibit buildings, house-
museums with period
furnishings, and craft
demonstrations.*

NORTH DAKOTA

Three Affiliated Tribes
Museum
P.O. Box 220
New Town 58763
(701) 627-4477
*The museum houses a large
library and collections
representing the heritage and
culture of the tribes that inhabited
and still inhabit the region.*

OHIO

Dunham Tavern Museum
6709 Euclid Avenue
Cleveland 44103
(216) 431-1060
*Historic house built in 1824,
with period furnishings.*

The Massillon Museum
212 Lincoln Way East
Massillon 44646
(216) 833-4061
*Changing collections of
American folk art exhibited in a
historic 1835 house.*

Schoenbrunn Village
Box 129
New Philadelphia 44663
(216) 339-3636
*Re-created late-18th-century
Native American village with 19
log structures, burial grounds,
and church.*

The Shaker Historical Society
Museum
16740 South Park Boulevard
Shaker Heights 44120
(216) 921-1201
*Collections of 19th-century
Shaker furniture of the North
Union Colony and Eastern
communities.*

OKLAHOMA

Ataloa Lodge
Bacone College
Muskogee 74401
(918) 687-3878
*Collections of spears,
arrowheads, Navajo rugs,
pottery, and baskets.*

Creek Council House
Museum
Town Square
Okmulgee 74447
(918) 756-2324
*A National Historic Landmark
dedicated to the preservation and
collection of all materials relating
to the Muskogee Creek Tribe.*

OREGON

Aurora Colony Historical
Society
Second and Liberty Streets
Aurora 97002
(503) 678-5754
*Three historic dwellings—the
Ox Barn Museum, Kraus
House, and Steinbach Cabin—
associated with the Aurora
Colony, a communal society
founded in 1856.*

Dr. Henry John Minthorn
House
115 South River Street
Molalla 97038
(503) 538-2831
*The pioneer Quaker house,
belonging to his uncle, where
President Hoover grew up.*

Mission Mill Museum
Mill Street
Salem 97301
(503) 364-4019
(503) 585-7012
Includes several mid-19th-century buildings: the Jason Lee House, Methodist Mission Parsonage, John D. Boon House, Mission, and Thomas Kay Woolen Mill.

Robert Newell House
8089 Champoeg Road NE
Champoeg 97137
(503) 678-5537
A reconstructed residence of 1852, with authentic furniture from Oregon's pioneers. Exhibits include pioneer quilts and Native American baskets.

PENNSYLVANIA
Brandywine River Museum
U.S. 1
P.O. Box 141
Chadds Ford 19317
(215) 388-7601
A museum located in a century-old grist mill, with paintings by the Wyeth family, Howard Pyle, Maxfield Parrish, Frank Schoonover, and others.

Daniel Boone Homestead
R.D. 2
Birdsboro 19508
(215) 582-4900
A mid-19th-century farmhouse, blacksmith shop, and barn built on the foundations of the birthplace of the American pioneer.

Philadelphia Museum of Art
26th Street and Benjamin Franklin Parkway
Philadelphia 19103
(215) 763-8100
Collections include Pennsylvania German artifacts, the Millbach Pennsylvania German kitchen, native paintings from the Garbisch Collection, and Shaker artifacts.

William Penn Memorial Museum
North and Third Streets
Harrisburg 17120
(717) 787-4978
Collections of 17th-, 18th-, and 19th-century Pennsylvania decorative arts, with permanent and special exhibits.

Wright's Ferry Mansion
38 South Second Street
Columbia 17512
(717) 684-4325
Restored 18th-century house with Pennsylvania William & Mary and Queen Anne furniture.

TENNESSEE
Center for Southern Folklore
1216 Peabody Avenue
Memphis 38104
(901) 726-4205
Artifacts, contemporary folk art, and crafts from the 20th-century South.

Great Smoky Mountain National Park
Gatlinburg 37738
(615) 436-5615
One hundred 18th- to early-20th-century log cabin structures, with pioneer museum and mill demonstrations.

The Hermitage
Rachel's Lane
Hermitage 37076
(615) 889-2941
Built in the early 19th century, this was the cotton plantation home of Andrew Jackson and his wife. It contains the original family's furnishings, and is situated on over 600 acres with lovely flower gardens.

Museum of Appalachia
Box 359, Highway 61
Norris 37828
(615) 482-3481
Several reconstructed and furnished log cabins, including a blacksmith's shop, corn-grinding mill, smokehouse, broom and rope factory, and display barn with frontier and pioneer memorabilia.

TEXAS
Bayou Bend Collection
Museum of Fine Arts
1 Westcott Street, Box 13157
Houston 77019
(713) 529-8773
Twenty-two rooms of American decorative arts from the 17th to the 19th century.

Henkel Square Restoration
P.O. Box 82
Round Top 78954
(713) 622-4889
Authentic representation of the life of early German settlers in Texas; includes pre–Civil War houses with period furnishings.

Winedale Historical Center
University of Texas at Austin
P.O. Box 11
Round Top 78954
Center for the study of the ethnic cultures of central Texas. A 190-acre farmstead with original house and outbuildings; three additional pre–Civil War buildings.

VERMONT
The Bennington Museum
West Main Street
Bennington 05201
(802) 442-2180
Collections of American crafts, folk art, furniture, Grandma Moses paintings, early American glass, and Bennington pottery.

Shelburne Museum
U.S. 17
Shelburne 05482
(802) 985-3346
Collections of Americana, including early American houses, shops, a steamboat, a covered bridge, folk art exhibits, textiles, costumes, dolls, decoys, and toys.

Sheldon Museum
1 Park Street
Middlebury 05753
(802) 388-2117
A house built in 1829 contains collections of pewter, toys, pottery, 18th- and 19th-century furnishings, tools, and 19th-century oil portraits.

VIRGINIA
Colonial Williamsburg
P.O. Box C
Williamsburg 23185
(804) 229-1000
Re-created 18th-century colonial town, including shops, houses, public buildings, and gardens.

Jamestown Island
Jamestown 23081
(804) 898-3400
Interpretation of the first permanent English settlement in the New World of 1607.

Mary Washington House
1200 Charles Street
Fredericksburg 22401
(703) 373-1569
Home of George Washington's mother, built in 1772, with 18th-century furnishings.

Mount Vernon
Mount Vernon 22121
(703) 780-2000
Historic home of George Washington. Exhibits include family furniture, paintings, a greenhouse, and gardens.

WEST VIRGINIA
Harpers Ferry National Park
Harpers Ferry 25425
(304) 535-6371
Nineteenth-century restored historic old business district of Harpers Ferry and site of the famous pre–Civil War raid of John Brown and his abolitionist followers.

WASHINGTON
Fort Vancouver National
   Historic Site
Vancouver 98660
(206) 696-7655
Partial reconstruction of important farming and manufacturing community and fur trade capital, with stockade and buildings as they appeared in the 1840s.

WISCONSIN
Milton House
16 South Janesville
Milton 53563
(608) 868-7772
Restored inn dating from 1844, with collections of Native American and pioneer relics and 1837 log cabin.

Stonefield
Cassville 53806
(608) 725-5210
Agricultural museum with 1890s replica of pioneer village and 19th-century Nelson Dewey house and grounds.

WYOMING
Buffalo Bill Historical Center
720 Sheridan Avenue
P.O. Box 1000
Cody 82414
(307) 587-4771

Index